Dappled

Dappled

BAKING RECIPES FOR FRUIT LOVERS

Nicole Rucker

AVERY

an imprint of Penguin Random House
New York

AVERY

an imprint of Penguin Random House LLC
penguinrandomhouse.com

Most Avery books are available at special quantity discounts for bulk purchase
for sales promotions, premiums, fund-raising, and educational needs.
Special books or book excerpts also can be created to fit specific needs.
For details, write SpecialMarkets@penguinrandomhouse.com.

Library of Congress Cataloging-in-Publication Data

Names: Rucker, Nicole, author.
Title: Dappled : baking recipes for fruit lovers / Nicole Rucker.
Description: New York : Avery, an imprint of Penguin Random House, [2019] |
Includes index.
Identifiers: LCCN 2018058468| ISBN 9780735218017 (hardcover) |
ISBN 9780735218024 (ebook)
Subjects: LCSH: Desserts. | Cooking (Fruit) | Baking.
Classification: LCC TX773 .R84 2019 | DDC 641.86—dc23
LC record available at https://lccn.loc.gov/2018058468
p.   c.m.

Printed in the United States of America
1 3 5 7 9 10 8 6 4 2

Book design by Ashley Tucker

For Blaine Rucker,
my tolerant, loving,
and brilliant husband

CONTENTS

Introduction 9

How to Choose Fruit 13

Fruit for Breakfast and Brunch 17

Cookies and Bars 61

Dessert Cakes, Puddings,
Cobblers, and Crisps 77

Pies, Tarts, and Galettes 135

Ice Creams and Sorbets 187

Sugared, Salted, and Preserved 205

Pantry Recipes 231

Acknowledgments 249

Index 251

Introduction

Once when I was a little girl, maybe seven years old, I was left to roam in my grandparents' garden while the adults prepared Sunday lunch. I remember noticing the perfect cherry tomatoes cascading on vines, the leaves glowing with sticky essential oils. They called to me, and I responded by grabbing them two at a time and gobbling them up, replaying that hedonistic call and response until I had eaten everything within arm's reach. I vaguely remember a seed of knowledge planting in my tiny brain—the realization that there were things, outside things, that I could eat. I simply had to find them.

That day, the whole yard came into focus and I began to search for anything I could eat. I didn't have to wait for some grown-up person to wash, cut, or cook. I could graze there as long as I was left alone to forage.

This was the start of my obsession with fruit. I was a hungry child with a good imagination, and I made a game out of finding anything free and edible. My sister, Tracy, and I cased entire neighborhoods, planning our walk to school around front yards with tangerine or lemon trees, patches of Oxalis flowers (sour grass), and landscaping with wild strawberries as ground cover. Sometimes we didn't even eat the things we foraged; we were just proud that we were able to find them. We collected kumquats like junk hoarders, usually leaving them on a bench or sidewalk later that day for someone else to notice.

Occasionally food was scarce in our house. This could be one more reason I started making note of alternate sources of food outside of the kitchen. If we had nothing in the cupboards, I felt more secure knowing that I knew where to find avocados beyond the grocery store's produce aisle. If we needed to find food, I could find it. I played kitchen, the way all little kids do, with pretend tea parties and restaurants. I loved watching the adults cook, and stuck close to them to begin collecting recipes and techniques.

When I was a teenager, and a latchkey kid, I spent a lot of my afternoons drawing and daydreaming in the backyard of our house. I had been baking banana bread and Nestlé Toll House cookies for years, but I'd become fixated on the fruits growing in the backyard that my mom didn't have time to care for and enjoy. I harvested apricots, plums, and warm-weather apples from that yard. I became enraptured by the peach tree in the corner of the lot, and the green beetles that buzzed around it and me as I picked what fruit I could save from the birds and other creatures—those that owned the tree more so than myself. I think we lived in that house only two years. I was sad to leave the trees behind. I didn't bake a peach pie until I was in my twenties.

I credit my grandparents on my mother's side for teaching me the basics of eating and cooking. I can picture my grandpa John gathering hot peppers and tomatoes from the garden and bringing them to the kitchen, to my grandma Camille, where she charred their skins over the flame on the stove. The smell of the peppers is so vivid as a memory, it makes my heart swell just writing this. She then placed the blackened things in a bowl and covered them with plastic wrap to sweat some of the char off before making a salsa. Grandpa grew it, he brought it inside, she transformed it. There was a comforting rhythm in those steps that I would crave to reenact as I became an adult.

I went to art school and studied photography. I began making cakes and cookies for friends. I took pictures of the cakes I made, obsessed with documenting my creations. I spent more time in the art school café than I did in the darkrooms. (For many years, the San Francisco Art Institute had one of the best college cafés in the country.) One day I spent my last two dollars on an Elberta Peach and had another wide-eyed moment with a piece of fruit that threw the future into focus. I realized I liked making cakes better than taking pictures of them and decided to become a baker.

I read every book I could afford on baking and pastry. Once I began working in restaurants, I learned that market day was the best day, like Christmas each week, but the day before market day was the most important test of your talent. Did you have enough berries to get through service? Had you overordered expensive plums, their once-taut skins now showing the wrinkles of overripeness? What about the broken and bruised figs?

Could you turn them into something delightful?

This is my favorite part of working with fruit, the daydreaming and planning that goes into using every last piece before it's too late, before the market truck shows up at the kitchen door and the next precious variety of perfect pears comes in. With fruit, there is a schedule you are minding. Upon each variety and crate that comes through the door there is a clock ticking away, whispering "use me, eat me, or else."

Seasons are not so obvious here in Southern California. Depending on where you call home, you may have a defined schedule of weather that marks actual seasons, or you may have a weird calendar of blurred lines like we do in Los Angeles. Is it fall in October? L.A. in the fall can mean 80°F to 100°F, and ice cream and salads. There are Halloween pumpkins on porches with candles melting right out of their ghoulish mouths, and we still have peaches at the farmer's markets. It's very confusing.

For this reason, I have not written a book structured strictly around seasonality. I prefer to encourage you to think more like a professional baker, to use what is available to you and to use it all.

In the pages that follow, you'll find a collection of fruit-forward recipes. Many of the recipes can be made with any fruit, such as the Pear Shrub, Fruit Crisp or Crumble but Not Cobbler, and the Sweet Wine and Fruit Cake. Others are careful flavor combinations meant to highlight a fruit and accompanying flavors (July Flame Peach Pie, Flourless Chocolate and Pear Spoon Cake).

I'm in love with fruit, because fruit can be magically complex. I am in love with fruit because it teaches me something new every season. I hope you will be inspired by what is abundant, and extract every last drop of juice and every lesson it holds.

How to
Choose Fruit

How it usually works: You bought the most delicious, ripe peaches at the farmer's market. When you arrive home, you realize they have been bashed up in transport, as if someone threw them at a wall, and are now effectively peach baby food in your bag. If it was a particularly hot day, they may have even fermented in the bag, which can happen in a matter of hours under the right conditions (microbes on the fruit's skin + warm plastic bag + repeated jostling).

Anyone who has shopped a farmer's market has done this. I have done this. It's a real bummer, especially because those perfect peaches, figs, or strawberries were not cheap! If you understand ripeness, and how a traditional display of produce at the farmer's market works, you can prevent tragic fruit bashing.

Is it ripe?

Ripening happens due to the production of naturally occurring chemicals, enzymes, and hormones in fruit, such as ethylene gas, pectinase, amylase, and kinases. These molecules are each responsible for different parts of the transforma-

tion from inedible to edible. A burst of ethylene gas accelerates the ripening process. Pectinases help to dissolve fruit pectin, creating softness and juiciness. Amylase gets to work on mealy starches and turns them into sugar, creating sweetness. Kinases in fruit contribute to making astringent acid into flavors more palatable, or remove acidity altogether. In the final stage of ripening, large organic molecules break down into smaller molecules, which creates more intense aromas. (This is my favorite part. Open a box of ripe pears one day, and you'll smell heaven.)

Bruising or cutting fruit can speed up the ripening process, which is why tender peaches thrown about in a bag will turn for the worse very quickly. This is also why "one bad apple spoils the bunch." A damaged apple quickly begins to release ethylene gas, and every apple around it will respond to the gas and ripen with it.

Fruits can be separated by their ripening process into two categories: those that will continue to ripen on the table and those that must ripen on the vine/branch. Fruits that continue to ripen are said to have a climacteric—a noticeable rise in respiration just prior to full ripening that allows for oxygen to be taken in and carbon dioxide to be released through the cells. During the process, heat and water are also produced. Fruits that have a climacteric have longer shelf lives than those without, as they can be controlled by environment. Knowing the difference between the two categories can be useful to you when you purchase fruits.

Fruit that will continue to ripen after picking or purchase (those with a climacteric)

Apples and Quinces	Dates	Peaches
Apricots	Honeydew	Pears
Avocados	Kiwi	Persimmons
Bananas	Mangos	Plums
Cantaloupe	Nectarines	Tomatoes
	Passion fruits	

When choosing fruits from this category, it's best to plan ahead for a mix of ripe and almost ripe. Bring a sturdy box or reusable container to protect fruits with softer skins from being damaged on the trip home. Tote bags are cute, but I have been scolded by my favorite avocado farmer for trying to drop some precious Pinkerton avocados into my bag—and rightfully so, I know better! If you can get your hands on a farmer's cardboard fruit box, keep it for as long as it holds up. Placing a sheet of parchment or craft paper in the bottom will help protect the box from any juices that will eventually damage the box. The boxes farmers use are meant to transport, store, and continue ripening the fruit. That's why they have air holes, which allow for the flow of air that both helps the ripening process along and prevents a buildup of gases that expedite mold and rotting.

Once purchased or picked, bring your fruits home from the market and assess the situation—remove everything from plastic bags or containers. Rinse the fruits under cool water and pat them gently with a clean towel to remove excess water. Arrange the fruits in a single layer with a little space between each piece of fruit, giving the fruits room to breathe. The space makes for even ripening and is another way to prevent premature molding. I like to use rimmed baking sheets lined with paper to lay out all my fruits from ripest in the front to least ripe in the back. A large cake plate with a mesh cloche is also a nice presentable way to store fruits on the table or kitchen counter.

Most of the fruits from this category can be stored at room temperature for several days, and the flavors and aromas will increase over that time. Once the fruits hit their peak in aroma, they can be eaten right away or stored in the fridge. In the case of quinces, persimmons, passion fruits, and tomatoes, storing them at room temperature can be done for as long as two weeks, and even longer in certain climates, depending on light/temperature/humidity.

Fruit that must be harvested ripe (those without a climacteric)

Blackberries	Figs	Pumpkins
Blueberries	Grapes	Strawberries
Cherries	Pineapples	Watermelons
Citrus	Pomegranates	

Many of my favorite fruits are on this list, but I have been disappointed by them all, as I am sure you have as well. These fruits are elusive with their peak ripeness and depend heavily on patient farmers who determine *just* the right time to harvest them and bring them to market. Your raspberries will not get sweeter with time. If they were picked too soon, they will get softer only by decay.

An unripe fig will break down and get juicier over the week, but it will not get sweeter or more complex. Most people who live in North America have never tasted truly ripe pineapples, which should be on every fruit lover's bucket list because they are incredible. They are, sadly, a rare find because ripe pineapples and other fragile ripe fruits do not travel well from the point of origin to the market.

If you are buying from a farmer's market, or even a friendly supermarket that offers samples, taste the fruit before buying. Berries in particular need to be sampled; color is not always the final word on ripeness, and for strawberries specifically. With strawberries, I rely more on aroma, as I have read that what we perceive to be flavor is actually a complex blend of hundreds of vapor molecules that create the experience of a ripe strawberry flavor. The most important thing to remember about this category of fruit is that the softer members of the group are fragile.

Berries, figs, cherries, and grapes at the peak of ripeness are very fragile and should be carefully transported. Once home, store the fruits in a single layer at cool room temperature or place them in the fruit/veggie drawer in your fridge. Berries and figs should be covered when placed in the fridge to prevent them from drying out. They can be kept at cool room temperature for a day as long as they're away from direct sunlight. Protect your investment; this category of fruit is usually the most expensive. It's for good reason, when you take into account the labor and time involved in growing and harvesting only ripe fruits and ones with a short shelf life.

If you can find some space in your life to grow one edible thing, even just one pot or tree that can be nurtured, do it. A lot of the fruits my husband and I grow don't even make it into baked goods or cooked meals. They are eaten while grazing in the yard (except tomatoes; there are always too many tomatoes). My favorite thing to grow for myself are tiny alpine strawberries. They are so small and I get only a handful at a time, but they're so packed with flavor that they're worth it.

If you can grow a citrus tree at home, it will be one of the most rewarding gifts you give yourself. If you can grow apples in your growing zone, I am jealous of you and I hope you take advantage of that ability and plant a couple of varieties. Wherever you are, I hope you find the recipes in this book inspiring and useful for making the most of whatever fruit can be found nearby. That is my wish for you.

Fruit for Breakfast and Brunch

Raspberry Scones

Apricot Bostock

Berry and Bran Muffins

Multi-Grain Porridge and Pear Pancakes

Dutch Baby with Sautéed Apple Compote

Fruit Soup

Strawberry Brioche Danishes
    with Fromage Blanc

Jam-Filled Doughnuts

Strawberry Rye Buckle
    with Rose Hazelnut Crumb

Rhubarb Coffee Cake
    with Browned Butter Streusel

Banana Buckwheat Cake

Plum and Yogurt Soufflé Cake

Apricot Almond Polenta Cake

Carrot and Pineapple Cake
    with Coconut Glaze

Avocado Pistachio Pound Cake
    with Lemon Glaze

Fermented Banana Cake

Mango Coconut Bundt Cake

Sour Lemon Cakes

Sweet Corn and Raspberry Muffins

Raspberry Scones

Makes 16 scones

4¾ cups plus 2 tablespoons (610g) all-purpose flour, plus more for rolling

1 tablespoon baking powder

½ cup (100g) granulated sugar

1¼ teaspoons kosher salt

2 sticks plus 5 tablespoons (297g) unsalted butter, cold and cut into ½-inch cubes

¾ cup (177ml) buttermilk

1 cup (236ml) heavy cream

2 cups (250g) frozen raspberries

Turbinado sugar, for sprinkling (optional)

This versatile scone recipe can be made using pretty much any fruit, fresh or dried. Softer fruits like pumpkins and bananas should be avoided, as well as overripe fruits.

1. Line two baking sheets with parchment paper.

2. In a large mixing bowl, sift the flour and baking powder. Add the granulated sugar and salt and whisk to combine. Add the cold butter and cut the butter into the flour mixture using a pastry blender or your hands to make a crumbly mixture with visible chunks of butter throughout.

3. In a measuring cup, combine the buttermilk and ¾ cup of the heavy cream. Slowly drizzle half the buttermilk mixture over the flour and butter mixture. Use your hands to incorporate the wet into the dry by fluffing then gently squeezing the scone dough together.

4. Add the rest of the buttermilk mixture and continue fluffing and squeezing until all the dough has been moistened by the liquid. Add the frozen raspberries and gently incorporate them into the shaggy, loose dough—be gentle with the berries. Bring the dough together into a rough mass and let it rest for 5 minutes.

5. Transfer the dough to a lightly floured work surface. Gather and pat the dough into an 11 x 7-inch rectangle, about 1 inch thick. Fold the dough in half to make a square, and use a rolling pin to roll the dough out again to a 1-inch-thick rectangle. Use flour as needed to prevent sticking. Fold the dough over again on itself to make a square, and transfer it to one of the prepared baking sheets. Cover the baking sheet in plastic, and chill for 20 minutes.

6. Position two racks in the center zone of your oven and preheat the oven to 400°F.

7. When the dough is chilled, use the rolling pin to roll it out to an 11 x 7-inch rectangle and use a sharp knife to cut the rectangle into eight rectangles, four across and two down, then cut each rectangle in half diagonally to make 16 triangles. Place the scones about 2½ inches apart on the prepared baking sheets. Brush the tops of the scones with the remaining ¼ cup heavy cream and sprinkle them with turbinado sugar, if desired.

8. Place the scones into the oven and reduce the temperature to 375°F. Bake until golden brown, 25 to 30 minutes, rotating the baking sheets top to bottom and front to back halfway through. Let the scones cool slightly on the baking sheets on wire racks. Serve warm or at room temperature.

Apricot Bostock

Makes 6 pieces

brandy syrup

¼ cup (50g) sugar

1 teaspoon vanilla bean paste or extract

2 tablespoons brandy, whiskey, or rum

to assemble

12 fresh ripe apricots

6 slices brioche, each about ½ inch
  thick, toasted

1 recipe Almond Cream (page 247)

¾ cup (69g) sliced almonds

Confectioners' sugar, for serving

Apricot bostock has all the richness of the best almond croissant with less than half the work. The apricot is a bright contrast to the buttery, nutty base of brioche toast slathered in almond cream. It's an impressive way to transform a simple loaf of bread into a decadent brunch (or dessert!) dish.

1. **Make the syrup:** In a small saucepan, combine the sugar, vanilla, and ¼ cup (59ml) water. Bring to a simmer over medium-high heat, stirring constantly. When the sugar has dissolved, after about 5 minutes, remove from the heat. Stir in the brandy. Let the syrup cool to room temperature.

2. **Assemble the bostock:** Cut each apricot into quarters, removing the pits. (Reserve the apricot pits for another use, like Brown Sugar Apricot Kernel Ice Cream; page 189.)

3. Position a rack in the center of your oven and preheat the oven to 400°F. Line a baking sheet with parchment paper.

4. Arrange the brioche toasts on the prepared baking sheet. Thoroughly soak each one with the brandy syrup. Spread a layer of almond cream about ¼ inch thick on each toast.

5. Arrange the apricots on top of the almond cream, using 8 slices of fruit per toast. Gently press the fruit into the almond cream so it stays in place, and top the fruit with a scant tablespoon more almond cream. Sprinkle the sliced almonds over the toasts.

6. Bake until the almonds and almond cream are deep golden brown, 15 to 20 minutes. Dust with confectioners' sugar before serving. Bostock keeps well in a sealed container at room temperature for up to 3 days.

note: Almonds and apricots is my favorite combination, but this recipe can be made with any fruit. Plums, berries, Slow-Cooked Rhubarb (page 208), and pears are all worthy substitutions.

Berry and Bran Muffins

Makes 12
standard-size muffins

1 stick (113g) unsalted butter, melted, plus more for greasing

15 (106g) fresh Medjool dates, pitted

1 cup (236ml) boiling water

1 cup (120g) whole-wheat flour

¾ cup (94g) all-purpose flour

2 teaspoons baking soda

1 teaspoon baking powder

1 teaspoon ground cinnamon

2 teaspoons kosher salt

1 large whole egg plus 1 large egg yolk

⅔ cup (133g) packed dark brown sugar

½ cup (118ml) grade A dark maple syrup

1 teaspoon vanilla bean paste or extract

2 cups (450g) full-fat plain yogurt

2 cups (116g) wheat bran

2 cups (220g) fresh or frozen blueberries

¼ cup (63g) turbinado sugar

note: Nearly any berry or fruit can be used in these versatile muffins. My favorite is blueberries, but chopped apples, bananas, apricots, and prunes are also great in this recipe.

This is the recipe to sway the hearts of haters who give side-eye to bran muffins. Berries and dates may draw the bran muffin skeptics in, but the secret to this recipe's success is the mellow, warming sweetness of maple syrup and the tenderizing properties of full-fat yogurt. These muffins are even better the day after you make them, which is some kind of witchcraft I can't explain.

1. Position a rack in the center of your oven and preheat the oven to 400°F. Butter a 12-cup standard-size muffin pan, or line with individual muffin papers.

2. Combine the dates and the boiling water in a small heatproof bowl. Cover the bowl with plastic wrap and let it stand until the dates are very soft and fall apart easily, about 10 minutes. Mash the dates and hot water together to create a gooey, chunky mixture.

3. Sift the whole-wheat flour, all-purpose flour, baking soda, baking powder, and cinnamon together in a large mixing bowl. Add the salt and any bran from the whole-wheat flour that was caught in the sifter to the flour mixture; set aside.

4. Whisk the egg and egg yolk together in another large bowl until well combined. Add the brown sugar, maple syrup, and vanilla; whisk vigorously until the mixture is pale and well aerated. Add the melted butter, yogurt, and dates and whisk to combine. Stir in the wheat bran and let the mixture sit until the bran is evenly moistened, about 5 minutes.

5. Add the wet ingredients to the flour mixture and fold to combine until no dry bits of flour remain. Add the blueberries and fold them into the batter gently, until they are distributed evenly throughout.

6. Divide the batter evenly among the prepared muffin cups. Do not level or flatten the surfaces of the muffins. Sprinkle each muffin with 1 teaspoon turbinado sugar.

7. Bake the muffins for 10 minutes, rotate the pan 180°, and reduce the temperature to 375°F. Continue baking until a cake tester inserted into the center of a muffin comes out with only a few crumbs attached, 16 to 20 minutes. Cool the muffins in the pan for 5 minutes, then transfer to a wire rack and cool for 10 minutes more before serving. These muffins keep well in a sealed container at room temperature for up to 1 week.

Multi-Grain Porridge and Pear Pancakes

Makes 4
thick 8-inch pancakes

⅓ cup (30g) old-fashioned rolled oats

⅓ cup (60g) kasha (toasted buckwheat groats)

4 ripe pears, such as Forelle, Bartlett, or Anjou

2 tablespoons granulated sugar

2 cups (240g) whole-wheat flour

¼ cup (50g) packed dark brown sugar

2 teaspoons baking powder

1 teaspoon baking soda

1 teaspoon ground cinnamon

1 teaspoon kosher salt

1 tablespoon poppy seeds

1 tablespoon golden flax seeds

2 cups (472ml) buttermilk

2 large eggs, lightly beaten

4 tablespoons (56g) unsalted butter, melted, plus more for cooking and serving

Maple syrup, for serving

So much of baking today is far removed from the smell, taste, and texture of the grains used to make flour. This pancake recipe is an antidote to homogenization of grains. Find the freshest flour, oats, and buckwheat you can get your hands on for this recipe. You will be able to taste the difference in the first bite.

1. Combine the oats, kasha, and 1½ cups (354ml) water in a medium saucepan. Cook, uncovered, over medium heat until the kasha is tender and the grains have cooked down to a thick porridge, about 30 minutes. Remove the pan from the heat and cool the porridge for at least 1 hour or overnight. You can make the porridge ahead of time and store it in the fridge until you are ready to make the pancakes.

2. Position a rack in the center of your oven and preheat the oven to 350°F. Cut the pears, remove the core using a melon baller or a teaspoon, and cut into ½-inch-thick slices. Combine the pear slices with the granulated sugar; set aside.

3. Put the whole-wheat flour, brown sugar, baking powder, baking soda, and cinnamon in a large mixing bowl and whisk to combine. Add the salt, poppy seeds, flax seeds, and any bran from the whole-wheat flour that was captured in the sifter to the bowl. Whisk to combine.

4. Make a well in the center of the flour mixture, and add the buttermilk, eggs, melted butter, and the porridge. Beat vigorously until no dry bits of flour or grains remain.

5. Heat two 10-inch pans (ovenproof nonstick or cast-iron) over medium heat. Lightly butter each pan and arrange one-fourth of the pear slices in each one. Top the pears with one-fourth of the batter, spreading the batter over the fruit. Cook undisturbed until you see several bubbles form on the surface, 1 to 2 minutes. Place the pans in the preheated oven and bake until a toothpick inserted into the middle comes out clean, 15 to 20 minutes. Transfer each pancake to a plate, and serve with butter and maple syrup, or keep warm. Wipe the pans clean and repeat with the remaining pears and batter.

6. You can make these pancakes one by one, as well; the batter does not suffer from waiting for the other pancakes to cook. The pancakes can be kept warm or reheated in the oven once taken out of the pan.

note: The porridge needs to be made ahead of time and cooled for at least 1 hour. You can make the porridge up to 1 day in advance.

Dutch Baby with Sautéed Apple Compote

Makes one 10-inch pancake

sautéed apple compote

2 large tart and firm apples, such as Granny Smith, Pink Lady, or Mutsu

2 tablespoons fresh lemon juice

¼ cup (36g) dried currants

¼ cup (59ml) grade A dark maple syrup

2 tablespoons salted butter

dutch baby

4 large eggs

¾ cup (177ml) whole milk

½ cup (63g) all-purpose flour

¼ cup (50g) granulated sugar

½ teaspoon kosher salt

2 tablespoons salted butter, plus more for serving

Confectioners' sugar and lemon wedges, for serving

Once while on a trip to Tokyo, my husband and I indulged in a late-night treat at our hotel—a Dutch baby served with glossy cooked apples and delicious fresh butter. This is my version of that memory.

1. **Make the compote:** Peel the apples and remove the cores. Shred the apples on the largest-gauge holes of a box grater. In a medium bowl, toss the shredded apples with the lemon juice, dried currants, and maple syrup. Melt the butter in a medium saucepan set over medium heat. Add the apples and currants and any liquid from the bowl. Reduce the heat to low and gently cook the apples until they are tender and the liquid in the pan has evaporated, about 10 minutes. The apples will look shiny and be a little sticky. Set aside.

2. **Make the Dutch baby:** Position a rack in the center of your oven and preheat the oven to 425°F.

3. In a blender, combine the eggs, milk, flour, granulated sugar, and salt. Blend on high until very foamy, about 1 minute.

4. Over medium heat, melt the butter in a 10-inch cast-iron or ovenproof nonstick pan. Pour the batter into the pan and place in the oven. Bake the Dutch baby until it has puffed and ballooned up in the center and around the edges and is lightly browned, about 20 minutes.

5. Serve the pancake immediately, in the pan, topped with the sautéed apple compote and some salted butter. Dust with confectioners' sugar and squeeze with lemon.

Fruit Soup

½ cup (65g) dried apricots

½ cup (75g) dried mission figs

1 cinnamon stick

2 lemon slices

½ cup (100g) tapioca pearls, soaked
   in 3 cups water for 2 hours

½ cup (100g) sugar

1 large tart and firm apple, such as
   Granny Smith or Mutsu

2 tablespoons golden raisins

1 tablespoon dried currants

Yogurt and granola, or fresh cheese and
   toasted bread, for serving (optional)

Fruit soup is not really a soup, it's more like a fruit-based tapioca pudding. When I was first served fruit soup by my mother-in-law, Ann Marie, I recognized it as chia pudding's older Swedish cousin. My mother-in-law serves it for dessert with fresh cream and a plate of butter cookies, but I think it's a perfect breakfast alongside some full-fat yogurt and a handful of granola.

....

1. In a medium saucepan, combine the apricots, figs, cinnamon stick, lemon slices, and 3 cups (708ml) warm water, and let the fruit soak for 5 minutes. Drain the tapioca and add it along with the sugar to the pot. Bring the mixture to a boil over medium heat.

2. Allow the soup to boil for 1 minute, then reduce the heat to low and let simmer, stirring often to prevent sticking, for 10 minutes.

3. Peel and core the apple. Cut it into ½-inch cubes and set it aside.

4. Check the tapioca for doneness by removing a few pearls with a heat-resistant spoon and cooling them off under cold running water. The pearls will change from opaque white to mostly clear. If the tapioca is tender and cooked through, remove the soup from the heat and incorporate the raisins, currants, and cut apple. If the test tapioca pearl still needs more cooking time, return the pot to the heat and continue to simmer until tender. I leave the cinnamon stick and lemon slices in the soup; it looks lovely for presentation, and the cinnamon stick will continue to give some flavor as it sits in the dish.

5. Transfer the soup to a heat-resistant dish and allow it to cool to room temperature before putting it in the refrigerator. Chill for 6 hours or overnight before serving.

6. Serve scoops of chilled fruit soup over yogurt and topped with granola, or alongside mild fresh cheese with toasted bread, if desired.

note: This recipe requires at least 6 hours of chilling time.

Strawberry Brioche Danishes with Fromage Blanc

Makes 12 danishes

1 recipe Brioche Dough (page 241)

All-purpose flour, for rolling

fromage blanc filling

1 cup (240g) fromage blanc cheese

1 cup (200g) sugar, plus more
   for sprinkling

1 large egg yolk

Pinch kosher salt

1 teaspoon vanilla bean paste or extract

1 pound (453g) strawberries, hulled
   and quartered

1 large egg

Strawberries are an easy fruit to love, admittedly, and best eaten out of hand, but sometimes during berry season you have too many strawberries and you need a recipe to use them all! Think of those beat-up berries that got too close to the basket and smooshed a bit. They deserve to be eaten, too. When you have a great, all-purpose brioche dough such as the one on page 241, you are steps closer to making good on the summer promise of eating all your berries, even the bruised ones. You can substitute two tablespoons of jam for the strawberries during the winter season.

1. Line two baking sheets with parchment paper.

2. After the overnight rest in the fridge, turn the brioche dough out onto a lightly floured surface. Divide the dough into 12 equal pieces and dust the top of each piece with flour.

3. Pick up a piece of dough and quickly use your thumbs to stretch the surface of the dough downward. Tuck the dough underneath to create a smooth, taut surface. Rotate the piece of dough a quarter turn and repeat the tucking motion so that you have created a smooth-shaped ball of dough. Place the dough ball on one of the prepared baking sheets and repeat with the rest of the dough. Each baking sheet will have 6 balls of dough.

4. Dust the tops of the dough balls with a little more flour and cover the baking sheets loosely with plastic. Place the baking sheets in a warm area (about 75°F) for about 1 hour, until the balls have risen and increased in size by half.

5. **While the dough proofs, make the filling:** In a large bowl, combine the fromage blanc, sugar, egg yolk, salt, and vanilla and beat vigorously with a whisk until very smooth and fluffy. Set aside.

recipe continues

note: In America, fromage blanc is a thick fresh cheese made from cow's milk. The texture resembles yogurt or light cream cheese, but is lower in fat. In Europe fromage blanc ranges in thickness and texture from loose yogurt to buttermilk, and is extremely perishable. If you are unable to get your hands on a tub, you can substitute cream cheese or American-made Neufchâtel in equal measure.

The dough for this recipe needs to be made 1 day in advance, and the recipe requires 1 hour of proofing time.

6. Position two racks in the center zone of the oven and preheat to 375°F.

7. When the dough has risen, remove the plastic wrap and use your thumb to press a 2-inch-wide indentation in the center of each ball of dough. Fill the crater in each piece with a scant 2 tablespoons of filling. Divide the strawberries evenly over the tops of the dough balls. Lightly beat the egg. Gently brush any exposed areas of dough with the beaten egg and sprinkle each with sugar.

8. Bake for 10 minutes, then rotate the baking sheets top to bottom and front to back and continue to bake until the danishes are deep golden brown, another 10 to 12 minutes. Let the danishes cool for at least 15 minutes and serve warm or at room temperature. They keep well in a sealed container at room temperature for up to 2 days.

Jam-Filled Doughnuts

....

Makes 12 doughnuts

....

All-purpose flour, for rolling

1 recipe Brioche Dough (page 241)

4 thick slices sourdough bread (stale is best)

1 recipe Simple Sugar Glaze (page 246)

1 quart (944ml) grapeseed or canola oil, for frying

1 cup plus 4 tablespoons (315ml) strawberry jam, pureed until smooth

Freshly fried doughnuts might be one of life's greatest food pleasures. They're definitely worth the trouble of making a dough from scratch and frying at home. For the filling, any type of jam will do. You can even substitute Olive Oil Lemon Curd (page 212) for jam if you'd like.

....

1. Line a baking sheet with parchment paper and lightly dust the paper with flour. Preheat the oven to 350°F.

2. After the overnight rest in the fridge, turn the brioche dough out onto a lightly floured surface. Divide the dough into 12 equal pieces and dust the top of each piece with flour.

3. Pick up a piece of dough and quickly use your thumbs to stretch the surface of the dough downward. Tuck the dough underneath to create a smooth, taut surface. Rotate the piece of dough a quarter turn and repeat the tucking motion so that you have created a smooth-shaped ball of dough. Place the dough ball on the prepared baking sheet and flatten it with your hand. Repeat with the rest of the dough.

4. Dust the tops of the dough with a little more flour and cover the baking sheet loosely with plastic wrap. Place the baking sheet in a warm area (about 75°F) for about 1 hour, until the balls have risen and increased in size by half.

5. While the dough rises, make the sourdough crumbs. Line a baking sheet with parchment paper. Tear the bread into chunks and put it in a single layer on the prepared baking sheet. Bake the bread until golden brown and dried out, about 25 minutes. Let the bread cool completely.

6. Transfer the chunks of dried bread to a plastic zip-top bag and use a rolling pin to crush them into crumbs. Pour the crumbs into a bowl and set aside. Transfer the simple sugar glaze to a large bowl.

7. Line a baking sheet with paper towels. In another baking sheet, place a wire rack. When the dough has risen, pour the oil into a heavy pot to a depth of 3 inches and heat to 375°F. Test the temperature of the oil with an instant-read thermometer. Fry 2 or 3 doughnuts at a time, dropping them gently into the oil and letting them fry on one side until the rapid bubbling subsides, about 1 minute.

recipe continues

8. Carefully flip each doughnut over with a slotted spoon, chopsticks, or tongs. Continue frying until the doughnuts are golden brown on both sides, 1 to 2 minutes more. Well-risen doughnuts will have a pale band around the middle. This is called the fry line.

9. Transfer the doughnuts to the paper towel–lined baking sheet to absorb any excess oil. While still hot, roll the doughnuts in the sugar glaze, then toss them immediately in the sourdough crumbs. Transfer the crumb-coated doughnuts to the prepared wire rack and let the doughnuts cool for 5 minutes. Repeat with the remaining uncooked doughnuts, working in small batches, and letting the oil reheat to 375°F before frying.

10. Fit a pastry bag with a small, round tip (about ½-inch) and fill it with the strawberry jam. Insert the tip into the top of each doughnut and pipe in a scant 2 tablespoons jam. Serve the doughnuts immediately; they are best eaten the same day.

note: The dough for this recipe needs to be made 1 day in advance and the recipe requires 1 hour of proofing time.

Strawberry Rye Buckle with Rose Hazelnut Crumb

....

Makes one 9-inch round cake

....

rose hazelnut crumb

½ cup (63g) all-purpose flour

¼ cup (40g) chopped toasted hazelnuts

¼ cup (50g) sugar

3 tablespoons grapeseed oil

1 tablespoon rose water

1 tablespoon dried, fragrant rose petals
(available at many natural foods
stores and online)

Rye flour contains less gluten than all-purpose wheat flour. Adding a bit of rye to a traditional buckle cake makes a delicate, nutty crumb that collapses in places under the weight of juicy berries. Cover that in hazelnut and rose petal crumble, and the humble buckle is elevated to the fanciest coffee cake.

. . . .

1. **Make the crumb:** In a medium bowl, combine the flour, hazelnuts, sugar, oil, rose water, and rose petals. Use a fork to mix until just combined. Squeeze a few handfuls of the sandy mixture for clumps. Cover the bowl and refrigerate while you prepare the cake.

2. **Make the buckle:** Position a rack in the center of the oven and preheat to 350°F. Butter a 9-inch round springform pan and line the bottom and sides with parchment paper.

3. Sift the all-purpose flour, rye flour, baking powder, and baking soda into a large bowl. Set aside.

4. In a measuring cup, combine the buttermilk and cream. Set aside.

5. In the bowl of an electric mixer fitted with the paddle attachment, beat the granulated sugar, butter, brown sugar, vanilla, and salt on medium speed until fluffy and very light in color, about 5 minutes. With the mixer running on low speed, add the eggs 1 at a time, mixing thoroughly after each addition. Scrape down the sides and bottom of the bowl.

6. Add the flour mixture and cream mixture to the batter in three additions, alternating between the two and mixing on low speed until no dry bits of flour remain.

buckle

Unsalted butter, for greasing

2½ cups (314g) all-purpose flour

2½ cups (255g) dark rye flour

½ teaspoon baking powder

½ teaspoon baking soda

1 cup (236ml) buttermilk

1 cup (236ml) heavy cream

1½ cups (300g) granulated sugar

1 stick plus 2 tablespoons (141g)
   unsalted butter, at room temperature

¾ cup (150g) packed dark brown sugar

1 teaspoon vanilla bean paste or extract

1 teaspoon kosher salt

4 large eggs

2 cups (332g) hulled and quartered
   fresh strawberries

2 tablespoons confectioners' sugar,
   for serving

7. Transfer half the batter to the prepared pan and top with half the strawberries. Press the fruit down lightly into the batter. Repeat with the remaining batter and berries. Scatter the crumb topping over the top, breaking up any large clumps of crumb.

8. Bake until a cake tester inserted into the center comes out clean, 45 to 50 minutes, rotating halfway through. Cool the cake completely in the pan, then remove from the pan and transfer it to a serving plate. Dust it with the confectioners' sugar. The cake will keep well in a sealed container for up to 3 days.

Rhubarb Coffee Cake with Browned Butter Streusel

Makes one 9 x 13-inch cake

Unsalted butter, for greasing

browned butter streusel
1 stick (113g) unsalted butter
½ cup (100g) granulated sugar
1 cup (125g) all-purpose flour
½ teaspoon kosher salt

cake
2 cups (250g) all-purpose flour
1 teaspoon baking powder
½ teaspoon baking soda
1 stick (113g) unsalted butter,
   at room temperature
1 cup (200g) granulated sugar
½ teaspoon kosher salt
2 large eggs
1½ cups (341g) full-fat plain
   Greek yogurt

In some parts of the world, rhubarb is the first "fruit" of the year, appearing in shades of pale pink while frost still permeates the ground. The best rhubarb is grown in dark barns and hothouses that are heated slowly to force the rhubarb from the cold earth. The darkness intensifies the ruby-red color when the peak of the season hits in mid-February and March.

....

1. Position a rack in the center of your oven and preheat the oven to 350°F. Grease a 9 x 13 x 2-inch baking pan and line the bottom and long sides with parchment paper.

2. Make the streusel: In a small, light-colored saucepan, bring the butter to a simmer over medium heat. Once the butter has melted, cook the butter, without stirring, until it begins to brown, about 4 minutes. The butter will foam a little; that's the sign that you are almost done. Once the butter is browned, and a nutty aroma wafts from the saucepan, remove the butter from the heat and transfer the browned butter and all the browned bits on the bottom to a heatproof mixing bowl. Cool to warm room temperature.

3. Combine the sugar, flour, and salt in a small mixing bowl. Add the browned butter and mix using a fork, until you have a crumbly, cereal-like mixture; set the streusel topping aside.

4. Make the cake: Sift the flour, baking powder, and baking soda into a small bowl.

5. In the bowl of an electric mixer fitted with the paddle attachment, beat the butter, sugar, and salt on medium speed until light and very fluffy, about 4 minutes.

6. With the mixer running on low speed, add the eggs 1 at a time. Mix thoroughly after each addition. Add the yogurt, vanilla, and candied citrus zest and mix until incorporated.

7. Still mixing on low speed, add the flour mixture to the batter in three parts, mixing after each addition just until no dry bits of flour remain. Transfer half the batter to the prepared pan and spread half the rhubarb over it. Cover the rhubarb with the remaining half of the batter. Drop the remaining rhubarb by the spoonful over the top of the cake.

recipe and ingredients continue

1 teaspoon vanilla bean paste
  or extract

½ cup (65g) Candied Citrus Zest,
  drained and chopped (page 211)

1 recipe Slow-Cooked Rhubarb
  (page 208)

8. Cover the cake with the browned butter streusel. Use all the streusel but do not press or pack the topping into the cake. Bake for about 45 minutes, rotating the pan halfway through, until the streusel is golden brown and a cake tester inserted into the center of the cake comes out with just a few moist crumbs clinging to it.

9. Cool the cake in its pan for 1 hour. Remove the cake from the pan and remove the parchment paper. Serve warm or at room temperature. The cake will keep well stored in a sealed container for up to 1 week.

note: Garden rhubarb can be found both fresh and frozen and can be used in the recipe with great success. The fruit won't have the same bright hue, but the flavor will still be bright and floral and cut through the browned butter topping. The slow-cooked rhubarb can be made well in advance and frozen for later use.

Banana Buckwheat Cake

Makes one 9 x 5-inch loaf cake

1¾ cups (235g) gluten-free flour blend

2 cups (240g) buckwheat flour

2 teaspoons baking powder

4 tablespoons golden flax meal

1 cup (236ml) extra-virgin coconut oil, plus extra for greasing the pan

2½ cups (375g) coconut sugar

2 cups (472ml) full-fat coconut milk, well shaken

2 teaspoons kosher salt

1 cup (200g) chopped toasted pecans

5 medium (510g) ripe bananas, chopped

½ cup (115g) chia seeds

Raw turbinado sugar, for sprinkling (optional)

This cake is gluten-, dairy-, and egg-free. In my experience, the main obstacle to gluten- and dairy-free baking has always been the desire to imitate the flavor and texture of wheat flour and butter. My solution is to embrace the character of the alternatives, enhancing their natural differences to create something new.

Here is an alternative to a traditional banana bread, made with coconut oil, coconut sugar, buckwheat flour, and a store-bought gluten-free flour blend. Look for a gluten-free flour that contains chickpea flour; it's the secret to this cake's moist and fudgy crumb.

1. Position a rack in the center of the oven and preheat to 350°F. Lightly oil a 9 x 5-inch loaf pan and line the bottom and long sides with parchment paper, leaving a ½-inch overhang.

2. Sift the gluten-free flour, buckwheat flour, and baking powder into a large mixing bowl; set aside.

3. Combine the flax meal with ¾ cup (177ml) warm water and set it aside.

4. Put the coconut oil in a small saucepan and warm it over low heat until it is melted. Combine the melted coconut oil, coconut sugar, coconut milk, and salt in a large mixing bowl and whisk vigorously until the mixture is emulsified and no dry bits of coconut sugar remain.

5. Make a well in the center of the flour mixture and add the wet ingredients and the hydrated flax meal. Mix just until combined. Add the pecans, bananas, and chia seeds and fold them into the batter until they are evenly distributed throughout.

6. Transfer the batter to the prepared loaf pan. Tap the loaf pan on the counter a few times to dislodge any air pockets. Sprinkle the top of the cake with turbinado sugar, if desired. Bake the cake until a cake tester inserted into the center of the loaf comes out with only a few moist crumbs clinging to it, 45 minutes to 1 hour.

7. Cool the cake in the pan for 30 minutes before gently lifting the paper and removing the loaf from the pan. Cool on a wire rack completely before cutting. This cake keeps well wrapped in plastic or in a sealed container for up to 1 week.

Plum and Yogurt Soufflé Cake

....

Makes one 9-inch round cake

....

Unsalted butter, for greasing

6 ripe medium plums (Satsuma, Damson, and Greengage are my favorites)

4 large eggs, separated into yolks and whites

½ cup (100g) sugar

1¾ cups (397g) full-fat plain Greek yogurt

3 tablespoons fresh lemon juice

1 teaspoon vanilla bean paste or extract

1 teaspoon kosher salt

½ cup (63g) all-purpose flour

½ teaspoon baking powder

1 cup Granola (page 233) or store-bought granola

note: This recipe can be made with any soft fruit. Berries, stone fruits, bananas, and ripe pears would all be excellent substitutions. If you desire to use apples or rhubarb in this dish, cook them ahead of time using the recipes on pages 207 and 208. Rehydrated dried fruit (dried fruit soaked in warm water or tea for 30 minutes), especially presoaked dried apricots, would also work.

You know those people who say they eat fruit pie or crisp for breakfast? This recipe is for them. Thick yogurt pudding with fruit and granola is baked, transforming the standard breakfast bowl into a fluffy soufflé. I'm not trying to sell this as being virtuous in any way, but it could make a fancy alternative to the typical weekend brunch yogurt cup.

....

1. Position a rack in the center of your oven and preheat the oven to 350°F. Butter a 9-inch round springform pan.

2. Pit the plums and cut each into 8 slices. Set aside.

3. Combine the egg yolks and ¼ cup of the sugar in a large mixing bowl. Beat vigorously until pale in color, you can use an electric mixer fitted with the whisk attachment for this if you want to. Add the yogurt, lemon juice, vanilla bean paste, and salt and whisk to combine.

4. Sift the flour and baking powder directly into the yogurt mixture and whisk until no dry bits of flour remain.

5. Place the egg whites in the clean and dry bowl of an electric mixer fitted with the whisk attachment. Beat on medium speed until foamy. Reduce the speed to low and, with the mixer running, slowly add the remaining ¼ cup sugar. Increase the speed to medium and beat until you have glossy, stiff peaks of meringue.

6. Incorporate the meringue into the yogurt mixture in three additions. Fold each addition into the batter until smooth, without streaks or clumps of meringue. Transfer the mixture to your prepared springform pan.

7. Arrange the plum slices on the surface of the batter. Scatter the granola over the top. Bake until the fruit has begun to caramelize and starts releasing some juices and the pudding has souffléd and browned at the edges, about 40 minutes.

8. Cool the cake for 20 minutes before removing the springform pan and transferring to a cake plate. Serve warm or at room temperature. This cake keeps well in a sealed container in the fridge for up to 2 days, but it's best eaten the same day.

Apricot Almond Polenta Cake

....

Makes one 9 x 5-inch loaf cake

....

Unsalted butter, for greasing

1 cup (125g) all-purpose flour

1 teaspoon baking powder

½ teaspoon baking soda

1 cup (96g) almond flour

½ cup (80g) fine-ground cornmeal

1 teaspoon kosher salt

3 large eggs

1 cup (200g) granulated sugar

1 cup (236ml) olive oil

6 fresh ripe apricots, pitted and cut into ½-inch slices

Turbinado sugar, for sprinkling

This is a sturdy cake packed with texture and flavor. Rich olive oil and almonds hug the tartness of apricots without eclipsing the fruit. This is a great cake to make and keep on the counter for a few days, as it holds up and makes a filling breakfast treat.

....

1. Position a rack in the center of the oven and preheat the oven to 350°F. Butter a 9 x 5-inch loaf pan and line the bottom and long sides with parchment paper, leaving a ½-inch overhang.

2. Sift the flour, baking powder, and baking soda into a large mixing bowl. Add the almond flour, cornmeal, and salt and whisk to combine.

3. In a separate bowl, beat the eggs and granulated sugar vigorously until light-colored and creamy; you can use an electric mixer fitted with a whisk attachment for this if you want, about 2 minutes. Add the oil in one continuous stream and beat until incorporated.

4. Make a well in the flour mixture and add the wet ingredients. Beat just until combined and no dry bits of flour remain.

5. Transfer the batter to the prepared pan. Arrange the apricot slices on top of the batter and sprinkle the entire cake with coarse sugar. Bake the cake until it is golden brown on top and a cake tester inserted into the center comes out with just a few moist crumbs attached, 45 to 50 minutes.

6. Let the cake cool in its pan for 30 minutes, then remove the cake by lifting the parchment paper, and carefully transfer it to a wire cooling rack. Let the cake cool completely before cutting. This will keep well in a sealed container at room temperature for 4 days.

note: This recipe is excellent made with rehydrated slab apricots—the sweetest and brightest-colored dried apricots that are cut in half before drying; they will often be flat and almost smashed looking compared to the other varieties of dried apricots. They retain a vibrant color and a concentrated apricot flavor, and can be very helpful during the winter when you need a cake with a little brightness to warm you up.

Carrot and Pineapple Cake with Coconut Glaze

Makes one 9 x 5-inch loaf cake

coconut glaze

One 14-ounce (414ml) can full-fat coconut milk, unshaken

¾ cup (94g) sifted confectioners' sugar

1 tablespoon dark rum (optional)

cake

Unsalted butter, for greasing

1¾ cups (210g) whole-wheat flour

1 teaspoon baking powder

½ teaspoon baking soda

¼ cup (40g) candied ginger, finely chopped, plus more for serving

¾ teaspoon kosher salt

¼ teaspoon ground nutmeg

1 tablespoon fresh grated ginger

1¼ cups (250g) packed dark brown sugar

½ cup (225g) pureed steamed or boiled carrots

½ cup (118ml) olive oil

2 large eggs

1 cup (150g) frozen or fresh pineapple chunks

This cake is sweet and spicy and brings back the old-fashioned tradition of putting pineapple in carrot cake. I love the gingery kick it has and the creamy coconut glaze, two twists to the traditional recipe. To make it more old-fashioned, you could add a handful of golden raisins or dried currants, which can be divisive but have always had a place in my heart.

1. **Make the coconut glaze:** Open the can of coconut milk, being careful not to shake the contents too much. Scoop out the cream of coconut that's settled at the top of the can. Combine the cream of coconut with the confectioners' sugar in a small bowl and whisk until combined. You will have a thick but smooth consistency. Add the rum, if using, or the coconut water, 1 teaspoon at a time, until you have a pourable consistency similar to runny honey; cover the bowl with plastic wrap and set aside.

2. **Make the cake:** Position a rack in the center of your oven and preheat the oven to 350°F. Butter a 9 x 5-inch loaf pan and line the bottom and long sides with parchment paper, leaving a ½-inch overhang.

3. Sift the whole-wheat flour, baking powder, and baking soda into a large mixing bowl. Add any bran captured by the sifter back to the bowl and add the candied ginger, salt, and nutmeg. Set aside.

4. Combine the fresh grated ginger, brown sugar, carrots, olive oil, and eggs in a blender or the bowl of a food processor fitted with the blade attachment and puree until very smooth.

5. Make a well in the center of the flour mixture. Add the contents of the blender and the pineapple and mix just until no dry bits of flour remain. Transfer the batter to the prepared pan. Bake the cake until a cake tester inserted into the center of the loaf comes out with only a few moist crumbs attached, 45 to 50 minutes. Allow the cake to cool to room temperature in its pan.

6. Once the cake has cooled completely, set a wire rack over a parchment-lined baking sheet. Remove the cake from the loaf pan by lifting the parchment paper at the sides. Transfer the cake to the wire rack and remove the parchment paper from the cake. Stir the coconut glaze well (it may have formed a crunchy layer on the surface—that's totally normal) and drizzle it over the cake. Decorate with dried pineapple slices, if desired, and candied ginger. Let the glaze settle for 20 minutes before cutting.

7. This cake keeps well in a sealed container at room temperature for up to 3 days.

Avocado Pistachio Pound Cake with Lemon Glaze

Makes one 9 x 5-inch loaf cake

cake

Unsalted butter, for greasing

2 cups (250g) all-purpose flour

1 teaspoon baking powder

½ teaspoon baking soda

¼ cup plus 2 tablespoons (40g) ground pistachios, unsalted and raw

½ teaspoon kosher salt

1½ cups (300g) granulated sugar

½ cup (118ml) grapeseed oil

2 large eggs

½ cup (200g) mashed, ripe avocado

½ cup (115g) sour cream

Zest of 1 large lemon

lemon glaze

½ cup (63g) confectioners' sugar

1 teaspoon freshly grated lemon zest

3 tablespoons fresh lemon juice

3 tablespoons ground pistachios

Candied lemon zest (page 211), edible flowers, and toasted pistachios, for serving (optional)

This cake feels to me 100 percent Californian, the land of abundant avocados. Use a good-quality avocado, and make sure it's not too ripe—just ripe enough to be sweet, and bright green where the flesh meets the skin.

1. **Make the cake:** Position a rack in the center of your oven and preheat the oven to 350°F. Butter a 9 x 5-inch loaf pan and line the bottom and long sides with parchment paper, leaving a ½-inch overhang.

2. Sift the flour, baking powder, and baking soda into a mixing bowl. Add the ground pistachios and salt and whisk to combine. Set aside.

3. In the bowl of an electric mixer fitted with the whisk attachment, beat the sugar, oil, and eggs together on medium speed until very light in color and creamy, about 2 minutes. Add the avocado, sour cream, and lemon zest and beat just until combined. Scrape down the sides and bottom of the bowl. Incorporate the flour mixture in three additions, mixing on low speed after each addition just until no bits of dry flour remain.

4. Transfer the batter to the prepared loaf pan and lightly rap the pan on the counter to dislodge any air pockets in the batter. Bake for about 1 hour, until a cake tester inserted into the center of the cake comes out with just a few moist crumbs attached. Allow the cake to cool completely in its pan.

5. **While the cake cools, make the glaze:** Sift the confectioners' sugar into a small mixing bowl. Add the lemon zest, lemon juice, and ground pistachios and mix until incorporated. The thickness should be similar to runny honey. If you want a thinner consistency, add water 1 teaspoon at a time and whisk until combined.

6. Set a wire rack over a parchment-lined baking sheet and turn the cake out onto the rack. Pour the glaze over the top. Decorate the cake with candied lemon zest, edible flowers, and candied pistachios, if desired. Let the glaze set on the cake for 20 minutes before cutting. This cake keeps well in a sealed container at room temperature for 1 week.

Fermented Banana Cake

....

Makes one 9-inch round cake

....

Unsalted butter, for greasing

2 cups (250g) all-purpose flour

1 tablespoon ground cinnamon

2 teaspoons baking powder

½ teaspoon baking soda

1 cup (230g) sour cream

1 cup (200g) packed dark brown sugar

1 cup Fermented Bananas (page 223)

½ cup (118ml) extra-virgin olive oil

¼ cup (59ml) honey

2 large eggs

1 teaspoon kosher salt

½ cup (29g) wheat bran

2 large bananas

Turbinado sugar, for sprinkling

In my opinion, bananas don't get the respect they are due. They're so often left bruised and speckled on the counters of corner stores, to be shoved into smoothies as a filler, or covered in pudding for banana cream pie (not hating on BCP, it's my favorite cream pie). Bananas are capable of so much more, and you will see the full range of banana flavor if you decide to devote a little extra time to your next bunch. Fermenting the bananas beforehand transforms the sugars of the ripe bananas into a tart, tropical-flavored mash that makes for a complex banana cake.

....

1. Position a rack in the center of your oven and preheat the oven to 350°F. Butter a 9-inch round springform pan.

2. Sift the flour, cinnamon, baking powder, and baking soda into a large mixing bowl. Set aside.

3. Combine the sour cream, brown sugar, fermented bananas, olive oil, honey, eggs, and salt in a separate bowl. Add the wheat bran and mix until no dry bits of bran remain. Allow the mixture to sit for 5 minutes before continuing.

4. Make a well in the center of the flour mixture and add the wet ingredients. Mix just until no dry bits of flour remain.

5. Transfer the batter to the prepared springform pan and lightly rap the pan on the counter to dislodge any air bubbles in the batter. Cut the fresh bananas diagonally into 1-inch-long slices. Arrange the banana slices on top of the batter and sprinkle the cake with turbinado sugar.

6. Bake until a cake tester inserted into the center of the cake comes out clean, about 45 minutes. Cool the cake completely in its pan. Remove the cake from the pan and transfer to a serving plate. Serve at room temperature. This cake keeps well in a sealed container or wrapped in plastic at room temperature for up to 3 days.

note: This recipe requires you to ferment the bananas up to 7 days in advance. Fresh bananas can be substituted in equal measure, with the addition of 1 tablespoon rum or whiskey to replicate the complex flavor of the fermented bananas.

Mango Coconut Bundt Cake

Makes one 9-inch,
10-cup bundt cake

2 sticks plus 2 tablespoons (254g) unsalted butter, at room temperature, plus more for greasing

4½ cups (563g) all-purpose flour

2 teaspoons baking powder

1 teaspoon baking soda

1 teaspoon vanilla bean paste or extract

½ teaspoon kosher salt

2¼ cups (450g) sugar

5 large eggs, separated into yolks and whites

1¼ cups (295ml) full-fat coconut milk, well shaken

2 large ripe mangos, peeled, pitted, and cut into 1-inch chunks

1 recipe Coconut Glaze (page 48)

Most good mangos should be eaten out of hand, over the sink, with a napkin nearby to mop up the mess that eating a mango like an animal makes. This is my preferred method for enjoying a mango, but every once in a while, I manage to save a good one and whip up this coconut cake. It makes an impressive brunch-table addition, but keeps well for a cake snack any time of day.

1. Position a rack in the center of your oven and preheat the oven to 350°F. Butter a 9-inch round Bundt cake pan.

2. Sift the flour, baking powder, and baking soda into a bowl. Set aside.

3. In the bowl of an electric mixer fitted with the paddle attachment, beat the butter on medium speed until glossy and smooth. Add the vanilla, salt, and sugar and continue to beat on medium until very pale in color and fluffy, about 5 minutes.

4. Reduce the speed to low and, with the mixer running, add the egg yolks one at a time, mixing thoroughly after every addition. Scrape down the bottom and sides of the bowl.

5. Incorporate the flour mixture and coconut milk in three additions, alternating between the two and mixing just until no dry bits of flour remain. Remove the paddle and bowl from the mixer, and transfer the batter to a large mixing bowl.

6. Thoroughly wash and dry the electric mixer bowl and add the egg whites. Fit the mixer with the whisk attachment and beat the egg whites on medium speed until soft peaks form. Add the egg whites to the batter in three additions, gently folding after each addition, until no streaks of egg white remain. Add the mangos and incorporate them into the batter.

7. Transfer the batter to the prepared pan. Bake the cake until a cake tester inserted into the center comes out with just a few moist crumbs clinging to it, about 1 hour, rotating the pan halfway through.

8. Cool the cake completely in its pan. Invert the cake onto a cake plate. Stir the coconut glaze and pour the glaze over the cake. Let the glaze settle for 20 minutes before cutting. This cake keeps well, stored in a sealed container for up to 1 week.

Sour Lemon Cakes

....

Makes 12 individual cakes

....

cakes

2 sticks plus 1½ tablespoons (245g) unsalted butter, at room temperature, plus more for greasing

1¾ cups (175g) cake flour

1 teaspoon baking powder

½ teaspoon kosher salt

1 cup (200g) sugar

3 large eggs

¼ cup (61g) full-fat plain yogurt

½ cup Olive Oil Lemon Curd (page 212)

1 tablespoon dark rum, whiskey, or brandy (optional)

1 teaspoon freshly grated lemon zest

3 tablespoons fresh lemon juice

lemon butter glaze

¾ cup (94g) confectioners' sugar

½ cup Olive Oil Lemon Curd (page 212)

3 teaspoons whole milk

Candied lemon zest (page 211) and edible flowers for decoration (optional)

note: This recipe requires lemon curd, which can be made in advance using the recipe on page 212, or substituted with store-bought lemon curd in equal measure.

These pretty little tea cakes are inspired by the British lemon drizzle cake. Tart and sweet, perfumed with fresh zest, for me they are the perfect afternoon snack. I like to use Eureka lemons for most of my baking, as they are nicely sour and they have a thick rind full of essential oils, but Meyer lemons are a lovely, mellow substitute if you have them—they produce a more floral aroma and a softer lemon tang.

. . . .

1. **Make the cakes:** Position a rack in the center of your oven and preheat it to 350°F. Butter a 12-cup muffin tin or lemon-shaped individual cake pan.

2. Sift the cake flour, baking powder, and salt into a mixing bowl and set aside.

3. In the bowl of an electric mixer fitted with the paddle attachment, beat the butter and sugar together on medium speed until light colored and fluffy, about 5 minutes. With the mixer running on low speed, add the eggs one at a time and mix thoroughly after each addition. Scrape down the sides and bottom of the bowl. Add the yogurt, lemon curd, rum, if using, lemon zest, and lemon juice and mix until incorporated.

4. Incorporate the flour mixture into the batter in three additions, mixing on low speed after each addition, just until no dry bits of flour remain. Divide the batter among the prepared muffin cups (a scant ¼ cup in each cup) and lightly rap the pan on the counter to dislodge any air pockets in the batter.

5. Bake the cakes until a cake tester inserted into the center of one of the cakes comes out clean, about 30 minutes, rotating the pan halfway through.

6. Cool the cakes in the pan on a wire cooling rack for 30 minutes. Set a wire rack over a parchment-lined baking sheet. Turn the cakes out onto the wire rack. Allow the cakes to cool completely before glazing.

7. **Make the lemon butter glaze:** Sift the confectioners' sugar into a small mixing bowl. Add the lemon curd and mix to combine. Add the milk 1 teaspoon at a time to thin the glaze to the consistency of runny honey.

8. Spoon the glaze over each cake and, if desired, top with candied lemon zest, edible flowers, or both! The cakes keep well in a sealed container in the fridge for up to 1 week.

Sweet Corn and Raspberry Muffins

Makes 12 muffins

2 ears yellow sweet corn, shucked and cleaned

1 stick (113g) unsalted butter, plus more for greasing

½ cup (118ml) whole milk

1¼ cups (156g) all-purpose flour

2 teaspoons baking powder

½ cup (80g) fine-ground yellow cornmeal

1 teaspoon kosher salt

2 large eggs

1 cup (200g) granulated sugar

Finely grated zest of 1 orange

3 cups (375g) fresh or frozen raspberries

Turbinado sugar, for sprinkling (optional)

These muffins get a ton of flavor from steeping the corn in milk, and it's worth the extra step when sweet corn is at its peak. This cake makes a superb base for strawberry shortcake, like the recipe on page 94.

1. Cut the kernels from the corncobs by cutting the tips off of the ears of corn, standing the ears on the flat ends, and running a sharp knife in between the kernels and the cobs. This is best done inside a shallow bowl or on a rimmed baking sheet.

2. In a large saucepan over medium heat, combine the corn with the butter and milk. Gently scrape the cobs with the back of a spoon over the saucepan to release any corn milk trapped inside. Discard the cobs. Heat the corn until the butter has melted and steam just starts to rise from the surface of the milk. Remove from the heat and let the corn cool to room temperature in the milk.

3. Position a rack in the center of your oven and preheat the oven to 375°F. Butter a 12-cup standard-size muffin pan, or line with individual muffin papers.

4. Sift the flour and baking powder into a bowl. Add the cornmeal and salt and whisk to combine. Set aside.

5. Combine the eggs and sugar in a large mixing bowl. Beat vigorously until the mixture is pale in color and creamy looking; you can use an electric mixer for this step if you want. Add the corn kernels and their milk along with the orange zest, and mix thoroughly.

6. Incorporate the flour mixture, mixing just until no dry bits of flour remain. Add the raspberries and gently fold in until they are well dispersed throughout the batter.

7. Divide the batter evenly among the prepared muffin cups and sprinkle the tops evenly with coarse sugar, if desired. Bake the muffins until a cake tester inserted into the center of one of the muffins comes out clean, 35 to 40 minutes. Cool the muffins in the pan to warm room temperature before diving in. They keep well in a sealed container for up to 1 week.

note: Any fruit can be used in these muffins. Especially delicious are berries, chopped peaches, or cooked rhubarb in equal measure.

Cookies and Bars

Raspberry Halva Brownies

Huckleberry Blondies

Candied Citrus Coconut Macaroons

Krystle's Lemon Ginger Cookies

PB&J Thumbprint Cookies

Pear Financiers

Pistachio Ginger Linzer Cookies

Cherry Almond Meringue Clouds

Chewy, Nutty, Fruity Granola Bars

Sour Cream Fig Bars

Raspberry Halva Brownies

....

Makes 12 brownies

....

2 sticks (226g) unsalted butter,
   plus more for greasing

1¼ cups (156g) all-purpose flour

2 tablespoons natural cocoa powder

1½ teaspoons kosher salt

10 ounces (283g) 72% cacao chocolate,
   chopped

1 ounce (28g) unsweetened baker's
   chocolate, chopped

¾ cup (150g) packed brown sugar

1½ cups (300g) granulated sugar

5 large eggs

1 cup (125g) fresh or frozen raspberries

6 ounces (170g) vanilla halva candy,
   cut into ½-inch cubes

note: Halva is a traditional confection from Middle Eastern cuisine that is made from sesame paste and sugar. In these brownies it has a softer, gentler peanut butter character. You can find halva candy in specialty food stores or online.

I'm not the kind of food person who describes edible things as sexy, that's not me, but I will admit to feeling things for these brownies. I think you could use them to woo someone successfully. They are that good. (See photo, page 60.)

....

1. Position a rack in the center of your oven and preheat the oven to 350°F. Butter an 8 x 12 x 2-inch baking pan and line the bottom and long sides with parchment paper, leaving a 1½-inch overhang at the sides.

2. Sift the flour, cocoa powder, and salt into a bowl. Set aside.

3. Fill a medium saucepan one-quarter full with water. Set over medium heat, and bring the water to a simmer. Combine the butter, 72% chocolate, and baker's chocolate in a very clean heatproof bowl and place over the simmering water. Stir gently until the butter and chocolate are melted and completely blended. Remove the bowl from the double boiler and place it on a dry towel.

4. In a large mixing bowl, combine the brown sugar, granulated sugar, and eggs. Beat vigorously with a whisk until the mixture is lighter in color and very creamy looking; you can use an electric mixer for this step if you want to. Add the chocolate mixture, and whisk to combine. Incorporate the flour mixture, mixing just until no dry bits remain.

5. Transfer the batter to the prepared pan and smooth the top. Scatter the raspberries and halva candy over the batter and gently press them into the surface. Gently rap the pan on the counter to dislodge any air pockets in the batter.

6. Bake for 10 minutes, rotate the pan, and continue baking until a cake tester inserted into the center comes out with very moist crumbs still clinging to it, about 20 minutes more. (I prefer to underbake these brownies. They will continue to carry-over cook while they cool, and the center brownies will set up nicely and become fudgey and toothsome rather than cakey.)

7. Remove the brownies from the oven and allow them to cool in the pan. Once completely cooled, carefully remove them from the pan by lifting the parchment paper at the sides. Cut into 12 brownies. Because of the raspberries, these brownies do not have the same shelf life as a standard bar cookie. They are best eaten within 3 days, but keep well in a sealed container in the fridge for up to 1 week.

Huckleberry Blondies

Makes 12 bars

1½ sticks (170g) unsalted butter, melted, plus more for greasing

1½ cups (188g) all-purpose flour

1 teaspoon baking powder

2 large eggs

1¾ cups (350g) packed dark brown sugar

1½ teaspoons kosher salt

1½ cups (200g) fresh or frozen huckleberries

Granulated sugar, for sprinkling (optional)

In their raw form, huckleberries can be underwhelming. They're tart with a subtle floral flavor. But when you cook or bake huckleberries, they are transformed into something remarkable. The color of the cooked fruit is a deeply saturated navy blue–purple, and the aroma is intoxicating. They pack a more intense flavor and aroma than their cousin the blueberry, but blueberries can be easily substituted cup for cup if you can't find huckleberries in your area.

1. Position a rack in the center of your oven and preheat the oven to 350°F. Butter a 9 x 13-inch pan and line the bottom and long sides with parchment paper, leaving a ½-inch overhang on the sides.

2. Sift the flour and baking powder into a bowl and set aside.

3. In a large mixing bowl, beat the eggs, brown sugar, and salt vigorously until the mixture is pale and thick; you can use an electric mixer for this if you want. Slowly drizzle in the melted butter and mix until well combined.

4. Incorporate the flour mixture in two additions, mixing after each addition just until no dry bits of flour remain. Add the huckleberries and gently fold them into the batter.

5. Transfer the batter to the prepared pan and spread it to the edges. Evenly sprinkle the top with granulated sugar, if desired. Bake for 10 minutes, rotate the pan, and continue to bake for about 15 minutes more, until a cake tester inserted into the center comes out with just a few moist crumbs clinging to it.

6. Remove the blondies from the oven and set the pan on a wire rack. Allow the bars to cool completely in the pan. Once completely cooled, carefully remove them from the pan by lifting the parchment paper at the sides. Cut the blondies into 12 bars or triangles and enjoy. They keep well in a sealed container at room temperature for up to 1 week.

Candied Citrus Coconut Macaroons

....

Makes 16 macaroons

....

⅓ cup plus 1 tablespoon (79g) sugar

¼ cup (59ml) honey

3 large egg whites

¼ cup (90g) Candied Citrus Zest—
whatever citrus is your favorite
(page 211), drained and diced into
confetti-like pieces

1 teaspoon vanilla bean paste or extract

½ teaspoon kosher salt

3 cups (245g) unsweetened shredded
coconut

2 tablespoons oil, for greasing

There is a sweet spot for achieving the perfect coconut macaroon, one that I have found most classic recipes miss. The texture should be crispy on the outside with a custardy, gooey inside. This is a difficult task, because shredded or flaked coconut is dried and will absorb a lot of the moisture. My method is to add the coconut to the gooey binder of egg whites and sugar, which starts the process of rehydrating the coconut. This will protect you from the dreaded dry macaroon.

....

1. Combine the sugar, honey, and egg whites in a medium saucepan and cook, stirring constantly, over low heat, until the sugar has dissolved, 3 to 5 minutes. Transfer the mixture to a heatproof bowl.

2. Add the candied citrus, vanilla, and salt to the egg mixture and stir to combine. Add the shredded coconut and fold in until all the coconut has been coated. Cool the batter to room temperature.

3. Position a rack in the center of your oven and preheat the oven to 325°F. Line a baking sheet with parchment paper.

4. Lightly oil your hands and shape the batter into 16 equal balls. Place them on the prepared baking sheet. Use your fingers to pinch-shape the balls of batter into little pyramids.

5. Bake the macaroons until they are golden brown on all sides, 15 to 20 minutes, rotating the tray halfway through. Allow the macaroons to cool on the tray until they are easily handled before peeling them off the parchment paper. They keep well in a sealed container for up to 1 week.

note: This recipe requires Candied Citrus Zest, which can be made in advance using the recipe on page 211. You can substitute store-bought candied citrus peel or the peel from thick-cut marmalade in equal measure.

PB&J
Thumbprint
Cookies

Krystle's
Lemon
Ginger
Cookies

Candied
Citrus
Coconut
Macaroons

Krystle's Lemon Ginger Cookies

Makes 36 cookies

2¾ cups (344g) all-purpose flour

1 teaspoon baking soda

½ teaspoon baking powder

1½ cups (300g) granulated sugar

2 sticks (226g) unsalted butter, very soft

1 large egg

Freshly grated zest of 4 large lemons

1 teaspoon vanilla bean paste or extract

½ cup (115g) chopped candied ginger

1 cup (250g) coarse sanding sugar

I have been truly blessed in my career to have worked alongside many generous and talented women. My sous chef Krystle Shelton is one of them, and her recipe for sugar cookies has always been my ultimate sugar cookie recipe. They are soft and chewy, and we make many variations of them throughout the year. Whether they're sprinkled with coarse sugar and scented with vanilla bean, rolled in rainbow jimmies, or chock-full of spicy ginger, I know that they will satiate any craving for cookie magic.

1. Position two racks in the center zone of your oven and preheat the oven to 350°F. Line two baking sheets with parchment paper; have more parchment paper at the ready for another round of baking.

2. Sift the flour, baking soda, and baking powder into a bowl. Set aside.

3. In the bowl of an electric mixer fitted with the paddle attachment, combine the sugar and butter and beat on medium speed until very fluffy and light in color, about 5 minutes. Add the egg and mix until fully incorporated and the mixture is smooth. Scrape down the bottom and sides of the bowl.

4. Add the lemon zest and vanilla and mix on low for 1 minute. Incorporate the flour in two additions, mixing after each addition just until combined. Add the chopped ginger and mix until the ginger bits are scattered throughout the dough.

5. Place the sanding sugar in a shallow dish. Use a portion scooper to scoop 36 balls of dough, about .75 ounces each (a #40 portion scoop is easily found online or in a local restaurant supply store and is perfect for this). Roll the dough balls in the sanding sugar. Place 12 cookies 2½ inches apart on each prepared baking sheet, reserving the rest of the dough in the fridge to bake later. Bake the two sheets of cookies for 5 minutes. Rotate the pans front to back and top to bottom, and continue to bake until the centers are set and the edges are golden, about 4 additional minutes. Remove the cookies from the oven and cool them completely on a wire rack.

note: **note:** This recipe is the perfect vehicle for any citrus zest, and it can take quite a lot of it. In winter I like to substitute pink grapefruit zest and a pinch of black pepper.

6. Unless you have a large home oven, or a double oven, you will need to cut and bake the cookies in batches, baking two sheets of cookies at a time. If you are reusing the same baking sheets, they will need to cool completely before continuing.

7. They keep well in a sealed container at room temperature for up to 1 week.

variations

Strawberry-Coconut: Replace the candied ginger with 2 cups freeze-dried strawberries and roll the cookies in unsweetened shredded coconut instead of the sparkly sanding sugar.

Orange-Anise: Replace the lemon zest with the zest of 2 large oranges. Add 2 teaspoons anise seed. Omit the ginger.

PB&J Thumbprint Cookies

....

Makes 24 cookies

....

2½ cups (313g) all-purpose flour

½ teaspoon baking powder

¼ teaspoon baking soda

1 teaspoon kosher salt

2 sticks (226g) unsalted butter, at room temperature

¾ cup (175g) smooth, natural peanut butter (unsalted)

¾ cup (150g) packed dark brown sugar

½ cup (100g) granulated sugar

1 teaspoon vanilla bean paste or extract

½ teaspoon almond extract

1 large egg

Coarse sanding sugar, for rolling

1 cup (300g) marmalade or jam

If you've been keeping count, you will notice that this is the sixth citrus recipe in this book. My only excuse is that I was told to write what I know, and I know and love citrus. If you're not a marmalade lover, feel free to ignore me and use another jam in these soft and salty peanut butter cookies. I highly recommend a guava or passionfruit jam, as they both pair shockingly well with peanut butter and they are less predictable than, say, strawberry. But strawberry is good, too! Just make the cookies.

....

1. Position two racks in the center zone of your oven and preheat the oven to 325°F. Line two baking sheets with parchment paper.

2. Sift the flour, baking powder, baking soda, and salt into a bowl and set aside.

3. In the bowl of an electric mixer fitted with the paddle attachment, beat the butter on medium speed until glossy and smooth. It should look like mayonnaise. Add the peanut butter, brown sugar, granulated sugar, vanilla, and almond extract and beat on medium speed until fluffy and very pale, about 5 minutes. Add the egg and beat to incorporate. Scrape down the bottom and sides of the bowl.

4. Add the flour mixture in three additions, mixing on low speed just until combined; scrape down the bottom and sides of the bowl in between additions and after all the flour has been incorporated.

5. Place the sanding sugar in a shallow bowl. Roll the dough into 1-inch balls. Roll each ball in the coarse sanding sugar and arrange on the prepared baking sheets, leaving about 3 inches between each cookie. Use your thumb or the back of a soup spoon to make a well in the center of each cookie. Fill each well with a generous teaspoon of marmalade.

6. Bake the cookies for 7 minutes, rotate the pans top to bottom and front to back, and continue baking until golden brown and set at the edges, about 4 additional minutes. Cool the cookies completely on a wire rack. Store the cookies in an airtight container for up to 1 week.

Pear Financiers

Makes forty-eight 2-inch cakes

2 sticks (226g) unsalted butter,
   plus more for greasing

¾ cup (94g) all-purpose flour,
   plus more for pan

1½ cups (300g) sugar, plus more
   for sprinkling

1½ cups (144g) almond flour, pistachio
   flour, or a mixture of the two

1 teaspoon kosher salt

7 large egg whites

1 tablespoon honey

4 firm-but-ripe pears, peeled and cored,
   cut into 1-inch cubes

note: This is one of the only recipes I advise using a silicone mold or nonstick pan for. It gives the financiers a shiny, caramelized exterior, unlike a traditional baking mold. They taste great with any fruit you can imagine substituted for the pears.

On the surface, a financier may appear to be "just another simple almond cake." If you look closely at the recipe and its simple ingredient list, you will notice that it's more of a ratio. One that results in a harmony of browned butter commingling with ground nuts and a healthy dose of salt. These cakes are baked in small molds, my favorite being a 2-inch half sphere, which makes them dangerously snackable.

1. Heat the butter in a large light-colored saucepan and bring it to a simmer over medium heat. Cook without stirring until the butter begins to brown, about 4 minutes. The butter will begin to foam a little just before the milk solids brown—that's the sign that you are almost done.

2. Once the butter has browned and a nutty aroma wafts from the pan, immediately remove the saucepan from the heat and transfer the butter to a heatproof bowl. Make sure to scrape the browned bits into the bowl as well. Do not strain them out. Let the butter cool for 5 minutes.

3. Position a rack in the center of your oven and preheat the oven to 350°F. Butter and flour a 24-cavity 2-inch half-sphere mold or 24-cup mini-muffin pan.

4. Place the sugar, almond flour, all-purpose flour, and salt into the bowl of an electric mixer fitted with the paddle attachment. Mix on medium speed until just combined.

5. Add the egg whites and honey to the mixer bowl and beat on medium speed until the whites are thoroughly incorporated. With the mixer on low speed, stream in the cooled browned butter. Increase the speed to medium and beat the batter until it is thick and glossy, about 4 minutes.

6. Spoon the batter into the mold or mini-muffin cups, filling each cavity three-quarters full. Sink 1 cube of pear into each cavity and sprinkle the top with sugar. Bake until the financiers just begin to rise, about 7 minutes. Rotate the pan and continue baking until the financiers are golden brown and the centers have set, about another 7 minutes.

7. Remove the financiers from the oven and unmold them immediately onto a wire cooling rack. Wipe any buttery residue from the mold, allow the mold to cool completely, and repeat with the rest of the batter. Store the little cakes in a sealed container for up to 3 days, or up to 1 week in the fridge.

Pistachio Ginger Linzer Cookies

Makes about 36 sandwich cookies

2 cups (250g) all-purpose flour, plus more for rolling

½ teaspoon baking powder

1 cup (150g) toasted shelled unsalted pistachios, ground into a coarse flour texture

½ teaspoon kosher salt

2 sticks (226g) unsalted butter, at room temperature

½ cup (100g) packed dark brown sugar

⅓ cup (79ml) dark molasses

1 tablespoon freshly grated lemon zest

1 tablespoon ground ginger

1 teaspoon ground cinnamon

½ teaspoon ground cloves

½ teaspoon ground white pepper

1 large egg

One 9-ounce (255g) jar pear preserves or apple butter

¼ cup (40g) chopped candied ginger

Confectioners' sugar, for serving

Pistachio Ginger Linzer Cookies are an idea spurred by the mind of Charlotte Druckman. One holiday season she was curating a group of recipes to reinvent the traditional Linzer cookie, and she asked me to participate. I combined two of my favorite cookies, the linzer and the molasses ginger, to make a spicy windowpane cookie filled with preserves. They're the perfect fancy treat to serve with strong black tea.

1. Sift the flour and baking powder into a bowl. Add the ground pistachios and salt and whisk to combine. Set aside.

2. In the bowl of an electric mixer fitted with the paddle attachment, beat the butter, brown sugar, and molasses together on medium speed until the molasses is totally incorporated into the butter and there are no visible streaks. Add the lemon zest, ground ginger, cinnamon, cloves, and white pepper and beat for 3 minutes. (Adding the spices to the fat and then beating them for a while allows the full flavor of the spices to work their way into the cookies.) Add the egg and mix until incorporated. Scrape down the bottom and sides of the bowl.

3. Incorporate the flour mixture in three additions, beating on low speed after each addition until no dry bits of flour remain. Remove the dough from the bowl and transfer it to a lightly floured surface. Gather the dough into a ball, cut the ball of dough in half, and flatten each half into a disc. Wrap each disc in plastic. Chill the dough in the refrigerator for 2 hours.

4. Position two racks in the center zone of your oven and preheat the oven to 325°F. Line two baking sheets with parchment paper.

5. Place the preserves and candied ginger in the bowl of a food processor and process until very smooth. Set aside.

6. Remove 1 disc of dough from the fridge. Allow the dough to sit at room temperature for 5 minutes, or until cold but semi-pliable—this is called tempering. Roll the dough between two sheets of lightly floured parchment paper to ⅛-inch thickness. (If the dough starts to become too sticky to roll, transfer it to a baking sheet and chill in the freezer for 10 minutes to firm it up.) Do not discard the leftover dough; simply gather it up into a disc and chill for 30 minutes. You can roll and cut more cookies once the dough has had some time to rest in the fridge.

recipe continues

note: You can use any thick jam in place of the pear preserves or apple butter. Raspberry would be traditional for a linzer, but apricot is a bright substitute.

This recipe requires that the dough be chilled for a minimum of 2 hours before baking. This can be done up to 3 days in advance.

7. Remove the top sheet of paper from the cookie dough and use a 3-inch round cookie cutter to cut out 24 cookies. Use a 1-inch round cutter to cut circles from the centers of half the cookies. Use an offset spatula to transfer 12 cookies to a prepared baking sheet, leaving 1 inch of space between each cookie. Freeze the cut-out cookies on the baking sheet for 10 minutes, or until firm, before baking.

8. Unless you have a large home oven, or a double oven, you will need to cut and bake the cookies in batches, baking two sheets of cookies at a time. If you are reusing the same baking sheets, they will need to cool completely before continuing.

9. Bake both sheets of cookies for 6 to 9 minutes, until the edges are golden. The cookies with the windowpanes cut out may bake a minute or two faster than the solid cookies; keep an eye on that. Let the cookies cool completely on the baking sheet, about 5 minutes.

10. Once the cookies have cooled, turn the solid cookies over and spread a generous teaspoon of preserves on the flat side. Top each jammed solid cookie with the flat side of a windowed cookie and dust with confectioners' sugar. Store the cookies in a sealed container in a single layer for up to 1 week.

Cherry Almond Meringue Clouds

Makes 12 large meringues

3 large egg whites

1 cup (200g) sugar

Pinch kosher salt

1 teaspoon apple cider vinegar

½ teaspoon almond extract

2 cups (184g) toasted sliced almonds

½ cup (85g) dried sour cherries

¼ cup (30g) natural cocoa powder

note: You can substitute any combination of chopped nuts and dried fruit in this recipe.

This recipe requires a baking time of 2½ hours.

One hot afternoon I decided to try to make these meringue cookies at home. At the time, we didn't own an electric mixer, something I ignored in the name of experimentation. I usually whisk whipped cream by hand, and I am a strong woman who regularly dead lifts sacks of flour with ease. Forty-five minutes (and four breaks) later, I had barely whisked them to soft ripples—maybe it was the humidity? I pressed on until I got something resembling thick marshmallow. My arms were exhausted. I was a mess. There was meringue on the wall. I persisted and was rewarded with a chewy, crunchy treat. Moral of the story: Do not attempt to make meringues by hand! Invest in an electric mixer. Even a handheld model will make the process much easier.

1. Position a rack in the center of your oven and preheat the oven to 250°F. Line a baking sheet with parchment paper.

2. In the bowl of an electric mixer fitted with the whisk attachment, beat the egg whites on medium-high speed until stiff peaks form. Slowly add the sugar and beat on medium speed until all the sugar has dissolved and silky peaks of meringue have formed. Add the salt, vinegar, and almond extract and beat on medium speed for 1 additional minute to combine.

3. Remove the bowl from the machine. Add the almonds and sour cherries and fold them into the meringue. Add the cocoa powder and fold in until the meringue has chocolatey streaks throughout. Do not mix the cocoa powder in completely.

4. Use a large serving spoon to scoop the meringues out onto the prepared baking sheet, leaving 1½ inches between them. There should be about 12, and they should each be the size of a medium lemon. Use your fingers or a fork to gently dig into the meringues on the tray and pull upwards to create more streaks and some swooping peaks. The peaks of the meringues will become crunchier than the centers during baking. This contrast of textures is the defining character of a well-made meringue cloud.

5. Lower the temperature of the oven to 200°F. Bake the meringues for 2½ hours, or until they are crisp to the touch on the outside and marshmallow-soft on the inside. Turn off the heat and let the meringues cool in the oven for 30 minutes. They are best eaten the same day, but they will keep well in a sealed container for up to 1 week.

Chewy, Nutty, Fruity Granola Bars

Makes 16 bars

Coconut or grapeseed oil, for greasing

1 cup (90g) old-fashioned rolled oats

1¼ cups (180g) whole unsalted roasted almonds

1 cup (160g) whole unsalted roasted peanuts

¾ cup (200g) toasted walnuts, coarsely chopped

¼ cup (50g) dried dates, pitted and diced

¼ cup (35g) dried strawberries, diced

½ cup (83g) golden raisins

1 tablespoon flaxseed meal

⅓ cup (79ml) honey

⅓ cup (79ml) brown rice syrup

½ teaspoon kosher salt

1 teaspoon vanilla bean paste or extract

These textural snack bars are virtuously high in fiber and protein, and are refined-sugar free. You can use any combination of dried fruits in this bar, or even freeze-dried fruit, to add an extra crunch.

. . . .

1. Position a rack in the center of your oven and preheat the oven to 350°F.

2. Lightly oil a large bowl, wooden spoon, and a 9 x 13-inch baking pan. Line the bottom and long sides of the pan with parchment paper, leaving a 2-inch overhang, and lightly oil the surface and sides of the paper.

3. Place the oats on a baking sheet and toast them in the oven, stirring them often to prevent burning, until lightly browned and fragrant, about 15 minutes.

4. Transfer the nuts and oats to the oiled bowl. Add the dried fruit and flaxseed meal, breaking apart clumps of fruit to distribute evenly throughout the mix.

5. Combine the honey, rice syrup, salt, vanilla, and ¼ cup (59ml) water in a 2-quart saucepan over medium heat and cook, stirring frequently, until the syrup reaches 260°F (hard-ball stage) on a candy thermometer, about 5 minutes. Immediately pour the honey syrup over the nut mixture and stir with the oiled wooden spoon until everything is evenly coated.

6. Transfer the mixture to the prepared 9 x 13-inch pan and use lightly oiled hands to spread it out evenly in the pan. Let the bars cool until they are set but still warm to the touch, then invert the pan onto a cutting board. Remove the parchment paper and cut into 16 bars. Store the bars in an airtight container at room temperature for up to 2 weeks or in your refrigerator for 1 month.

Sour Cream Fig Bars

Makes 12 bars

oat crumble crust

2 sticks (226g) unsalted butter, at room temperature, plus more for greasing

1½ cups (135g) old-fashioned rolled oats

1¾ cups (219g) all-purpose flour

1 teaspoon baking soda

1 cup (200g) packed dark brown sugar

sour cream fig filling

2 cups (300g) chopped dried mission figs

1 cup (236ml) hot brewed coffee

1 cup (200g) sugar

2½ teaspoons cornstarch

1½ cups (345g) sour cream

3 large egg yolks

½ teaspoon kosher salt

note: These bars keep very well in a sealed container stored at room temperature. To store them stacked, place parchment in between the layers of bars.

These versatile bars can be made with any dried fruit and any strong black tea in place of coffee. Traditionally they are made with raisins, which is the version my friend Rachael shared with me when I was on the hunt for a sturdy baked good I could pack up for a picnic. I swapped dried figs for raisins because that is what I had on hand, and I found dried figs and coffee make a great combination.

1. **Make the crust:** Position a rack in the center of your oven and preheat the oven to 350°F. Butter a 9 x 13-inch pan and line the bottom and long sides with parchment paper, leaving a ½-inch overhang on the sides.

2. Combine the oats, flour, and baking soda in a bowl and set aside.

3. In the bowl of an electric mixer fitted with the paddle attachment, beat the butter and brown sugar on medium speed until very light in color and fluffy, about 5 minutes. Scrape down the bottom and sides of the bowl. Add the flour mixture and beat on low speed until well combined.

4. Transfer half of the crumble to the prepared pan and press it into the bottom to form a crust. Reserve the other half at room temperature to use for the topping. Bake the crust for 7 to 10 minutes, until it has browned a little bit at the edges. Cool completely. Keep the oven on.

5. **Make the filling:** In a heatproof bowl, soak the dried figs in the hot coffee for 10 minutes, or until they are very soft. Drain the figs in a colander and discard the coffee. Allow the figs to drain for several minutes.

6. In a small saucepan, combine the sugar and cornstarch and mix them together with a fork (dispersing the cornstarch throughout the sugar helps prevent clumps). Add the sour cream, egg yolks, and salt. Mix until well combined. Cook, stirring constantly with a heatproof spatula, over low heat. Bring to a simmer and let the mixture thicken to a pudding. This should take about 7 minutes.

7. Remove the pudding from the heat and mix in the drained figs. Pour the filling into the cooled crust and crumble the reserved topping over the filling.

8. Bake until the topping is browned and the filling caramelizes at the edges of the pan, about 30 minutes. Remove the bars from the oven and allow them to cool in the pan. Once completely cooled, carefully remove the bars from the pan by lifting the parchment paper at the sides. Cut into 12 squares.

Dessert Cakes, Puddings, Cobblers, and Crisps

Spiced Tangerine Semolina Cake

Sweet Wine and Fruit Cake

Backyard Citrus Upside-Down Cake

Isabel's Lemon Birthday Cake

Spiced Apple Wedding Cake

Magic Banana Pudding Cake

Strawberry Cornmeal Shortcake

Swedish Cream Buns with Strawberries

Coffee and Croissant Bread Pudding

Flourless Chocolate and Pear Spoon Cake

Baked Vanilla Custard with Berries

Vanilla Rice Pudding
   with Marsala-Baked Pears

Passion Fruit Posset

Sweet Corn Pudding with Blackberries

Summer Pudding

Tomato Pudding

Pear and Ginger Strudel

Apple Brown Betty

Almond and Berry Cobbler

Peach and Ricotta Biscuit Cobbler

Fruit Crisp or Crumble but Not Cobbler

Rhubarb and Blood Orange Pavlova

note: Kishu tangerines are a tiny seedless variety with a ton of acidity and sweetness. You can substitute any lively tangerine variety if Kishus are not available in your area. Just make sure to choose something with great flavor and aroma, and avoid anything sprayed with wax. Alternately you can substitute oranges in equal weight.

Spiced Tangerine Semolina Cake

Makes one 9-inch round cake

cake

10 golf ball–size (375g) whole
  Kishu tangerines

Unsalted butter, for greasing

¾ cup (72g) almond flour

¾ cup (125g) coarse semolina flour

1 teaspoon baking powder

½ teaspoon kosher salt

6 large eggs

1¼ cups (250g) sugar

spiced syrup

1 cup (200g) sugar

1 piece star anise

1 cinnamon stick

2 tablespoons orange blossom water

to assemble

2 large Cara Cara oranges, segmented

3 Kishu tangerines, peeled and sliced
  into ¼-inch-thick circles

Is it possible to write a book about fruit and make no mention of the classic Claudia Roden recipe for whole orange and almond cake? Riffs on this recipe have been floating around since Roden first published *Middle Eastern Cooking* in 1987, and for good reason. It's a wonderfully smart recipe. Now I've thrown my hat into the ring with this spiced Kishu tangerine variation.

. . . .

1. **Make the cake:** Fill a large bowl with ice cubes and cold water. Place the tangerines in a large saucepan and cover them with cold water. Bring to a rolling boil over medium heat, reduce the heat to a simmer, and cook until fork tender, about 15 minutes. Transfer the tangerines to the ice bath.

2. Position a rack in the center of your oven and preheat the oven to 350°F. Butter a 9-inch round springform pan and line with parchment paper.

3. Drain the tangerines. Cut each in half and remove any seeds. Transfer the fruit to the bowl of a food processor fitted with the blade attachment. Process the tangerines into a moderately smooth puree.

4. Transfer the fruit puree to a large mixing bowl.

5. Combine the almond flour, semolina, baking powder, and salt in a small bowl. Whisk them together and set aside.

6. Add the eggs and sugar to the food processor and process until very frothy, about 5 minutes.

7. Add the egg mixture to the pureed tangerines and fold in until fully incorporated. Add the flour mixture in three additions, mixing just until combined after each addition.

8. Transfer the batter to the prepared springform pan and bake for 30 minutes without opening the oven door. Rotate the cake and continue baking for about 10 minutes more, until the center of the cake is bouncy but set when tapped gently with a finger and a cake tester inserted into the center of the cake comes out with just a few moist crumbs clinging to it. Cool the cake completely on a wire rack.

recipe continues

9. **While the cake cools, make the spiced syrup:** In a small saucepan, combine the sugar, star anise, and cinnamon stick with ¼ cup (59ml) water over medium heat. Bring the mixture to a simmer and cook, stirring, until the sugar dissolves completely, about 5 minutes. Remove the syrup from the heat and allow it to cool to room temperature. Add the orange blossom water. Discard the anise and cinnamon stick.

10. **To assemble:** Remove the cake from the pan and invert the cake onto a serving platter. Use a fork to poke a bunch of holes in the surface of the cake. Pour the spiced orange blossom syrup over the cake, soaking it. Arrange the citrus segments and slices on top and serve. This cake keeps well in a sealed container in the fridge for up to 1 week.

How to Eat an Orange

When I was a little girl, my parents both worked many different jobs to make ends meet in our house. They were creative. My mother was a singer in bands and made radio commercials. She was also a teacher and did graphic design. My father owned a print shop and sometimes worked on fishing boats. He was also a professional mime.

A vision of him as a mime comes to mind when I think about the first memory I have of sharing an orange with my dad. The way he peeled an orange for me, using his front teeth to break the skin and tear away the first strip of rind, was a performance. He started oranges for me because my fingers were too small and not strong enough to peel one on my own.

Eventually he encouraged me to start them myself this way. My first memory of that was biting into an orange rind and the spray of essential oils filling my nostrils. It was a full sensory experience. He could have started every orange with his thumbs, but I don't remember him ever doing that. I remember the exaggerated performance of his teeth gnashing into a navel orange like an animal on its prey.

Sweet Wine and Fruit Cake

....

Makes one 9-inch round cake

....

Unsalted butter, for greasing

½ cup (63g) all-purpose flour

1 teaspoon baking powder

1 teaspoon kosher salt

¼ teaspoon baking soda

1¼ cups (120g) almond flour

¾ cup (150g) sugar, plus more for sprinkling

½ cup (118ml) extra-virgin olive oil

2 large eggs

1 tablespoon orange marmalade or chopped Candied Citrus Zest (page 211)

½ cup (118ml) Beaumes-de-Venise or muscat dessert wine

½ pound (226g) dried black mission figs, quartered

½ cup (63g) muscat or champagne grapes

Freshly whipped cream, for serving (optional)

The scent of dessert wine wafting from the oven as this cake bakes is wonderfully complex. It smells rich and very grown-up. I usually avoid serving cakes with whipped cream, but this cake deserves it. This is an incredibly versatile base cake. You can use raspberries, pitted cherries, or fresh blackberries during the peak of summer. In the fall and winter months, pears and apples can be chucked in the batter, as well as dried apricots (the sunlight of the dried-fruit category).

....

1. Position a rack in the center of your oven and preheat the oven to 375°F. Butter a 9-inch round cake pan and line it with parchment paper.

2. Sift the all-purpose flour, baking powder, salt, and baking soda into a large mixing bowl. Add the almond flour and whisk to combine. Set aside.

3. Combine the sugar, olive oil, eggs, and marmalade in a blender or the bowl of a food processor and puree on high until the mixture has doubled in volume and is very light in color. Slowly, with the motor running, pour in the wine and blend just until the wine has been incorporated.

4. Make a well in the center of the dry ingredients and pour in the contents of the blender. Gently fold the batter together until no dry bits of flour remain. The batter will be very light and loose in texture, almost like pancake batter.

5. Transfer the batter to the prepared cake pan. Arrange the figs and grapes on the surface and sprinkle the fruit with sugar. Bake the cake until the surface has set and the color has just begun to brown, about 20 minutes. Rotate the cake and continue to bake until a cake tester inserted into the center comes out clean, about 30 minutes more. Let the cake cool to warm room temperature before removing it from the pan. Serve it with freshly whipped cream, if desired. This cake keeps well in a sealed container at room temperature for up to 2 days.

note: Beaumes-de-Venise is a region and also an AOC (Appellation d'Origine Contrôlée). You can substitute any white, sweet dessert wine made with muscat grapes if you are unable to find the specific wine from Beaumes-de-Venise.

Backyard Citrus Upside-Down Cake

I call this a "backyard cake" because in Southern California, and Los Angeles in particular, so many of us have a lemon, orange, or tangerine tree in our backyards. Sometimes they're in the front yard, or planted on the strip of land between the sidewalk and the curb, but you are never more than a block away from a citrus tree. The natural pectin in the citrus, combined with the sugar, creates a pudding-like upside-down layer that's similar to a buttery marmalade.

Makes one 9-inch round cake

upside-down layer

1 stick (113g) unsalted butter

½ cup (100g) plus 2 tablespoons sugar

2 large unwaxed lemons, ends trimmed, then halved, seeded, and sliced ⅛ inch thick

cake

2½ cups (313g) all-purpose flour

1 teaspoon baking powder

½ teaspoon baking soda

½ teaspoon kosher salt

2 large eggs

1 cup (236ml) olive oil

1 cup (227g) full-fat plain Greek yogurt

1 cup (200g) sugar

1. Position a rack in the center of your oven and preheat the oven to 350°F. Butter a 9-inch round cake pan and line it with parchment paper.

2. **Start by making the upside-down layer:** In a medium saucepan over low heat, melt the butter. Remove the pan from the heat and add ½ cup of the sugar and 2 tablespoons of water. Whisk the mixture until the sugar dissolves and the mixture is glossy and thickened a little. Pour the melted butter and sugar into the prepared cake pan and smooth into an even layer to cover the bottom. Place the cake pan in the freezer until the butter and sugar layer freezes; leave the pan in the freezer until you are ready to transfer the batter to the pan.

3. In a small bowl, gently toss the lemon slices with the remaining 2 tablespoons of sugar. Leave the lemon slices in the sugar to macerate for 10 minutes.

4. **While the upside-down layer freezes, make the cake batter:** Sift the flour, baking powder, baking soda, and salt into a large bowl. Set aside. Combine the eggs with the olive oil in another large bowl and beat vigorously with a whisk until well combined. Add the yogurt and sugar. Make a well in the flour mixture and add the wet mixture in three additions, folding in each addition until no dry bits of flour remain. Set aside.

5. Fan the lemon slices out to cover the melted butter and sugar in the cake pan, overlapping the slices by as much as ⅛ inch. Pour the cake batter directly on top of the lemon slices.

6. Bake for about 1 hour, until a cake tester inserted into the center comes out with only a few moist crumbs clinging to it. Transfer to a wire cooling rack and let cool for 15 minutes. Invert the cake onto a serving plate and carefully remove the parchment-paper lining. Allow the cake to cool for 1 hour more before serving.

note: This cake can be made with nearly any citrus, my favorite being lemon because I like it to be bitter and tart. The only citrus I would not use is raw grapefruit, oro blanco, or lime. The rinds of grapefruit and oro blanco are much thicker than lemons and oranges and they will take longer to bake. Lime and grapefruit also retain too much of the bitter quinine flavor and will make for an odd-tasting cake.

Isabel's Lemon Birthday Cake

....

Makes one 9-inch 3-layer cake

....

lemon cake

2 cups plus 2 tablespoons (266g) all-purpose flour

2 teaspoons baking powder

1½ teaspoons kosher salt

6 large eggs, yolks and whites separated

1½ cups (300g) sugar

1 cup (226g) Olive Oil Lemon Curd (page 212)

½ cup (118ml) olive oil

1 tablespoon lemon zest

lemon frosting

4 sticks (453g) unsalted butter, very soft

4 tablespoons lemon zest

4 cups (500g) confectioners' sugar

1 tablespoon whole milk

Edible flowers, candied lemon zest (page 211), and/or shredded unsweetened coconut, for decoration (optional)

My grandmother Isabel got the same cake for every birthday celebration. It was a lemon chiffon cake, filled with a faux lemon curd, covered in lemon frosting and shredded coconut. It was the cake of my youth; we never varied from the lemon flavor. I have loved lemon birthday cakes since, and I re-created the cake for my grandmother's ninetieth birthday. This recipe is for the most super-lemony cake you can imagine. It's a great cake to make for a winter birthday party, because despite their brightness in flavor and color, lemons are a winter fruit.

. . . .

1. **Make the cakes 1 day in advance:** Position a rack in the center of your oven and preheat the oven to 325°F. Butter three 9-inch round cake pans and line the bottom and sides with parchment paper.

2. Sift the flour, baking powder, and salt into a large mixing bowl. Set aside.

3. In a separate bowl, combine the egg yolks with the sugar and beat vigorously with a whisk until very light in color and creamy looking; you can use an electric mixer for this step if you want. Add ½ cup of the lemon curd, the olive oil, ½ cup (118ml) warm water, and the lemon zest. Whisk until well combined.

4. Make a well in the center of the dry ingredients and add the wet ingredients. Fold the batter together until no dry bits of flour remain.

5. Put the egg whites into the bowl of an electric mixer fitted with the whisk attachment and beat on medium speed until soft, glossy peaks form, about 3 minutes.

6. Incorporate the egg whites into the batter in three additions, folding gently after each addition. Carefully divide the batter between the three prepared pans. Bake for 20 minutes, rotate the pans, and continue to bake until a cake tester inserted into the centers of the cakes comes out clean and the tops are very lightly browned, about 10 additional minutes. Remove the cakes from the oven and place on a wire rack. Allow the cakes to cool completely in their pans before removing them and removing the parchment paper.

7. Wrap each cake layer in plastic and freeze the layers for at least 4 hours or preferably overnight.

recipe continues

note: You can substitute store-bought lemon curd if you are short on time and do not want to make your own from scratch. You will need approximately 16 ounces.

The cake layers should be made 1 day in advance to allow the cakes to freeze completely. It's best to freeze the cakes overnight before frosting them, as it makes the crumb more compact and easier to finish, and you can keep the cakes frozen for up to 2 weeks. This also makes frosting the cake much easier and results in a cleaner cake slice with defined layers. The frosting and filling should also be made in advance and can be stored, separately, for up to 1 week.

8. **Make the frosting:** Place the butter and lemon zest in the bowl of an electric mixer fitted with the paddle attachment. Beat on medium speed for 5 minutes, or until the butter is super shiny and smooth and smells intensely of lemon.

9. While the butter mixes, sift the confectioners' sugar into a medium bowl. Scrape down the bottom and sides of the mixer bowl and add one-third of the confectioners' sugar. Mix on low speed until the sugar has been fully incorporated. Scrape down the bottom and sides of the bowl and add the remaining two-thirds of confectioners' sugar; mix on low speed until all the sugar has been mixed in.

10. Once all the sugar has been incorporated, add the milk and beat on medium-low speed for 5 minutes, until smooth and billowy. The frosting can be stored at cool room temperature in a sealed container for 1 day. If your kitchen is very warm, store the frosting in the fridge and remove it 4 hours before you plan on assembling the cake.

11. **Assemble the cake:** When you are ready to assemble and decorate the cake, remove the layers from the freezer and remove the plastic wrap. Place 1 layer of cake on a serving plate or cake board and spread with ¼ cup of the lemon curd, leaving a ½-inch ring of cake uncovered at the edge.

12. Place your second cake layer on top of the first and repeat with the remaining ¼ cup lemon curd. Place the top layer on the cake, and gently press down on the center of the cake just a little bit.

13. Scoop a generous spoonful of frosting onto the top layer and spread it out and down the sides. Repeat until you have covered the cake. Use the back of a spoon or an offset spatula to swoop and swirl the frosting however you'd like. Decorate with edible flowers, candied lemon zest, and/or shredded coconut, as desired.

14. Store the cake in the fridge until 20 minutes before you are ready to serve it. It will keep well in a sealed container in the fridge for 1 week or in the freezer for 1 month (omit the flowers and other decoration until ready to serve, and defrost in the fridge overnight).

Spiced Apple Wedding Cake

*Makes one 9-inch round
4-layer cake*

spiced apple cake

Unsalted butter, for greasing

2¾ cups (344g) all-purpose flour

2 teaspoons ground cinnamon

1½ teaspoons baking powder

1 teaspoon baking soda

½ teaspoon ground nutmeg

½ teaspoon kosher salt

¼ teaspoon ground cloves

4 large eggs

1¼ cups (250g) granulated sugar

½ cup (100g) packed dark brown sugar

2 tablespoons unsulfured molasses

1½ cups (354 ml) extra-virgin olive oil

3 large (600g) Granny Smith, Pink
   Lady, and/or Fuji apples, cored and
   coarsely grated

2 tablespoons peeled and finely grated
   fresh ginger, about 2 inches

I first made this rustic wedding cake to celebrate two farmers who decided to marry in the fall. The wedding was attended by farmers from neighboring farms, and each brought vegetables, meat, and fruit to be used in the dinner party. I was given two large cases of huge green apples to spin into dessert, and this cake is the result. I decorated the cake with the tiniest crab apples dipped in hard caramel, husk cherries with the papers barely opened up, and fresh baby's breath. It is not your typical wedding cake. It's very deep in color and flavor.

1. **Make the cake:** Position a rack in the center of your oven and preheat the oven to 350°F. Butter two 9-inch round cake pans and line the bottoms and sides with parchment paper.

2. Sift the flour, cinnamon, baking powder, baking soda, nutmeg, salt, and cloves into a medium bowl and set aside.

3. In the bowl of an electric mixer fitted with the whisk attachment, beat the eggs, granulated sugar, brown sugar, and molasses together on medium speed until pale and thick, about 4 minutes. Reduce the speed to medium-low and gradually stream in the olive oil. Incorporate the flour mixture in three additions, mixing after each addition just until no dry bits of flour remain. Remove the bowl from the mixer and fold in the apples and ginger. Divide the batter between the prepared pans.

4. Bake the cakes for 30 minutes, rotate the pans, and continue to bake until a cake tester inserted into the centers of the cakes comes out clean, about 20 minutes more. Transfer the pans to a wire cooling rack and let the cakes cool for 20 minutes. Invert the cakes onto the wire rack. Let them cool completely, then stack them with their paper liners still attached (or new sheets of parchment in between each cake) and wrap in plastic. Freeze the cakes for 6 hours or overnight.

5. **Make the frosting:** Sift the confectioners' sugar into a bowl. Set aside.

6. In the bowl of an electric mixer fitted with the paddle attachment, beat the butter on medium speed until it is very smooth and shiny and looks like mayonnaise, 5 to 7 minutes. Add the vanilla and salt to the butter and beat until well combined. Reduce the speed to low and gradually incorporate the confectioners' sugar, beating the sugar and butter together until very fluffy, about 2 minutes. Scrape down the

recipe and ingredients continue

3½ cups (438g) confectioners' sugar

2 sticks (226g) unsalted butter,
    at room temperature

1 teaspoon vanilla bean paste or extract

Generous pinch kosher salt

Two 8-ounce packages (453g) cream
    cheese, at room temperature

Edible flowers, dried apples, and/
    or candied nuts, for decoration
    (optional)

bottom and sides of the bowl. Increase the speed to medium-high and add the cream cheese 1 tablespoon at a time. Once you've added all the cream cheese, scrape the bottom and sides of the bowl and then mix for 1 more minute.

7. **Assemble the cake:** When you are ready to assemble and decorate the cake, remove the layers from the freezer and remove the plastic wrap. Use a serrated knife to cut each layer in half horizontally to make 4 layers. Place 1 layer of cake on a serving plate or cake board and spread a generous scoop of frosting to the edge of the cake.

8. Place your second cake layer on top of the first and repeat with the frosting. Continue with the third and fourth layers. When you have placed the top layer on the cake, gently press down on the center of the cake just a little bit.

9. Scoop a generous spoonful of frosting onto the top layer and spread it out and down the sides. Repeat until you have covered the cake, then swoosh and swirl the frosting however you'd like, or scrape the sides down to reveal the sides of the cake, creating a "naked cake" look. Decorate with edible flowers, dried apples, and/or candied nuts as you wish.

10. The cake keeps well in a sealed container in the fridge for up to 1 week.

note: This recipe is for a 9-inch round 4-layer cake, but it can be easily scaled up to create a multi-tiered wedding cake. It's best to freeze the layers overnight before frosting them, as it makes the crumb more compact and easier to finish, and you can keep the cakes frozen for up to 2 weeks. This cake base also makes the best carrot cake. Substitute shredded carrots for apples in equal weight.

The cake layers should be made 1 day in advance to allow time to freeze them completely. This makes frosting the cake much easier and results in a cleaner cake slice with defined layers.

Magic Banana Pudding Cake

....

Makes one 8-inch round cake

....

1 stick (113g) unsalted butter, melted and cooled, plus more for greasing

¾ cup (94g) all-purpose flour

¼ teaspoon kosher salt

1 cup (236ml) Fermented Bananas (page 223)

2 tablespoons packed dark brown sugar

1 tablespoon dark rum or banana liqueur

1 teaspoon vanilla bean paste or extract

4 large eggs, yolks and whites separated

1¼ cups (250g) granulated sugar

2 cups (472ml) warm whole milk

Unsweetened whipped cream, for serving (optional)

note: You can substitute the Fermented Bananas in this recipe with 2 large ripe bananas.

This recipe requires at least 6 hours of chilling time.

Caramelized bananas flavored with dark rum create their own pudding-like layer in this "magic cake." The batter separates into three layers during the baking, and once completely cooled and sliced, it does look pretty magical.

....

1. Position a rack in the center of your oven and preheat the oven to 350°F. Butter an 8-inch round springform pan and line it with parchment.

2. Sift the flour and salt into a large mixing bowl. Set aside.

3. Combine the fermented bananas, brown sugar, rum, and vanilla in a large saucepan. Cook over medium heat, stirring frequently, until the bananas are slightly caramelized and the sugar has dissolved completely, 10 minutes. Remove the bananas from the heat and let cool until warm room temperature.

4. In the bowl of an electric mixer fitted with the whisk attachment, whip the egg whites on medium speed to very stiff peaks, about 4 minutes, and set aside.

5. In a large bowl, beat the melted butter, egg yolks, granulated sugar, and 1 tablespoon of water with a whisk until the mixture is very airy and light in color; you can do this step in an electric mixer if you want. Add the banana mixture and beat until well mixed.

6. Make a well in the center of the flour mixture and add the egg yolk mixture. Whisk until no dry bits of flour remain. Gradually add the warm milk and whisk until all of the milk has been incorporated.

7. Add the stiff egg whites to the batter in three additions, gently whisking after each addition. Stop mixing when the batter still has small bits of whipped egg white throughout. It won't be a fully incorporated batter; it will look a little rough and curdled.

8. Pour the batter into the prepared pan and bake, undisturbed, until the top is golden brown and the center still jiggles a little bit, about 40 minutes. Cool the cake completely in its pan on a wire rack. Wrap the cake in plastic while still in its pan and chill for 6 hours or overnight. Once chilled, remove the springform and parchment from the cake and serve with freshly whipped unsweetened cream, if desired.

9. This cake keeps well in a sealed container in the fridge for 3 days.

Strawberry Cornmeal Shortcake

....

Makes 6 generous portions

....

cake

Unsalted butter, for greasing

1 recipe Sweet Corn and Raspberry
  Muffins batter (page 59),
  without raspberries

to assemble

2 pounds (906g) fresh ripe
  strawberries, hulled and quartered

½ cup (100g) sugar

½ teaspoon vanilla bean paste
  or extract

Generous squeeze fresh lemon juice

Generous pinch kosher salt

2 cups (454g) full-fat plain Greek
  yogurt

2 cups (472ml) heavy cream

1 pint *fraises des bois* or other petite
  strawberry variety, for garnish
  (optional)

note: I don't bother with making
individual servings of this dessert. I like
to serve it in one big bowl, like a trifle
or mess, and let my guests scoop it for
themselves.

My mother's father, John Rodriguez, made sure that strawberry shortcake was on the menu any time his grandkids showed up for a meal. Sometimes he would sneak away just as we arrived to the house, and drive to the market to get the necessary supplies for his favorite dessert. My version is made with a fresh yogurt-whipped cream and a buttery corn cake base, which is a deviation from John's beloved Cool Whip and circular, individual sponge cakes, but it still gives me the warm fuzzies every time I eat it and think of him.

....

1. **Make the cake:** Position a rack in the center of your oven and preheat the oven to 350°F. Butter a 13 x 9-inch baking dish and line the bottom and long sides with parchment paper, leaving a 1-inch overhang.

2. Making sure to omit the raspberries, pour the prepared muffin batter into the prepared baking dish and bake for 30 minutes. Rotate the cake and continue to bake until a cake tester inserted into the center of the cake comes out with just a few moist crumbs clinging to it, about 15 additional minutes.

3. Allow the cake to cool completely in the pan on a wire rack.

4. **Assemble the dessert:** In a large bowl, combine the strawberry quarters with the sugar, vanilla, lemon juice, and salt. Cover the bowl and allow them to macerate at room temperature for 30 minutes.

5. In the bowl of an electric mixer fitted with the whisk attachment, combine the Greek yogurt and heavy cream. Beat on medium speed until you have smooth, soft peaks. Remove the bowl from the machine and manually whisk the cream two or three more times to create pronounced peaks.

6. Remove the cake from the pan and tear it into rustic, uneven chunks. Distribute half the cake pieces evenly across the bottom of a wide serving dish. Scatter the macerated berries over the cake pieces. Drizzle a few tablespoons of berry juice over everything. Dollop the cream on and in between the cake pieces. Repeat and layer with the remaining cake, berries, and cream. Garnish the surface with fraises des bois, if desired. There's no wrong way to arrange this dessert! Serve immediately.

Swedish Cream Buns with Strawberries

Makes 12 buns

1 recipe Brioche Dough (page 241)

All-purpose flour, for rolling

1 large egg

2 cups (472ml) plus 1 tablespoon heavy whipping cream

3 tablespoons Swedish pearl sugar or coarse sanding sugar

1 pound (453g) fresh strawberries, hulled and halved

3 tablespoons confectioners' sugar, plus more for rolling

1 teaspoon vanilla bean paste or extract

1 teaspoon ground cardamom

Swedish cream buns look like delicious clouds and taste like summer. They're second to strawberry shortcake on my list of favorite desserts. Can you think of anything dreamier than cardamom-scented whipped cream stuffed into a light, sweet brioche bun and adorned with strawberries? Whipped cream and fruit is a simple treat that appears in cuisines all over the world. In Japan, the cream bun becomes the "fruit sandwich," which is simply sliced brioche with whipped cream and fruit stuffed inside.

1. Line two baking sheets with parchment paper. After the overnight rest in the fridge, turn the brioche dough out onto a lightly floured surface. Divide the dough into 12 equal pieces and dust the top of each piece with a little flour. Pick up a piece of dough and use your thumbs to stretch and pull the surface of the dough downward. Tuck the dough underneath to create a smooth, taut surface. Rotate the piece of dough a quarter turn and repeat the tucking motion, then turn the piece over into the palm of your hand and pinch the bottom of the ball closed, so that you have created a smooth-shaped ball of dough. Place the dough ball on one of the prepared baking sheets and press down with your hand to flatten it a bit. Repeat with the rest of the dough balls, 6 buns per baking sheet, spaced 2 inches apart. Dust the tops of the buns with a little bit of flour and cover the baking sheets loosely with plastic wrap. Let the buns rest in a warm area (about 75°F) until they have risen and increased in size by half.

2. Position two racks in the center zone of your oven and preheat the oven to 375°F.

3. Beat the egg with 1 tablespoon of the cream to make an egg wash. Remove the plastic wrap from the buns and gently brush the top and sides of the dough with the egg wash. Sprinkle the buns with the pearl sugar. Bake for 10 minutes, then rotate the baking sheets top to bottom and front to back and continue to bake for another 6 to 8 minutes, until the buns are golden brown. Let the buns cool completely on the baking sheet set on a wire cooling rack.

4. Cut a 2-inch-wide, 1½-inch-deep crater into each bun with a paring knife. Reserve the bun tops and set aside. Place a strawberry half, cut-side up, into each crater and dust with confectioners' sugar.

recipe continues

note: If you are looking for a shortcut and don't want to spend a summer day making bread dough, find the best-quality brioche buns at your local bakery.

This recipe requires the Brioche Dough be made 1 day in advance.

5. In the bowl of an electric mixer fitted with the whisk attachment, combine the remaining 2 cups heavy cream, the 3 tablespoons of confectioners' sugar, the vanilla, and cardamom. Whip the cream on medium speed until soft peaks form. Remove the bowl and whisk attachment from the machine and whisk the cream by hand two or three times, until almost-stiff peaks form. The cream should be smooth but hold shape. Over-whipped cream will break down and end up clumpy; perfectly whipped cream will remain billowy and retain a smooth, tight texture even after being refrigerated.

6. Place the whipped cream into a pastry bag fitted with a ½-inch star tip. Pipe the cream into the buns, starting in the centers and working out and up to create a little height. Arrange the strawberry halves in a ring around the cream, cut sides facing in, to form a crown. If there is any space at the tops of the strawberry crowns, pipe a tiny bit of cream inside it. Place the cut-out bun pieces on top and dust with confectioners' sugar.

7. Serve immediately. Cream buns will keep well in the fridge for 1 day but are best eaten fresh.

Coffee and Croissant Bread Pudding

Makes 8 hearty portions

coffee custard

3 cups (708ml) heavy cream

2 cups (472ml) whole milk

2 teaspoons vanilla bean paste
  or extract

3 tablespoons instant espresso powder

2 large whole eggs plus 4 large
  egg yolks

1 cup (200g) packed dark brown sugar

½ teaspoon kosher salt

to assemble

Unsalted butter, for greasing

6 day-old croissants of any flavor
  (butter, almond, or chocolate),
  cut into 1-inch cubes

1 cup (150g) fresh blueberries

1 cup (235ml) strawberry jam

note: This recipe can be made with
2 double shots of cold espresso from your
favorite coffee shop if you do not have
instant espresso in your pantry. Simply
add the cooled espresso to the milk before
heating it.

This dessert can be served after dinner or for a decadent brunch. The flavors of croissants and coffee custard mimic breakfast, but are definitely more sumptuous than just a simple pastry and coffee. I have served this decadent pudding both warm and cold, and it's delicious both ways!

1. **Make the custard:** Combine the heavy cream, milk, and vanilla in a large saucepan and cook over medium heat until the mixture just begins to simmer, about 2 minutes. Remove from the heat, then add the espresso powder and whisk until the granules are dissolved. Allow the cream mixture to cool until it's room temperature.

2. Add the whole eggs, yolks, brown sugar, and salt to a large mixing bowl and beat with a whisk until the eggs are fully incorporated with the sugar. Add the cream mixture slowly, whisking until all of the egg mixture has been combined with the liquid.

3. **Assemble the bread pudding:** Butter a 9 x 13-inch baking dish. Arrange half of the croissant cubes in the prepared dish to cover the bottom. Scatter ½ cup of the blueberries over the cubes. Dollop half of the strawberry jam over the blueberries, 1 tablespoon at a time. Spread the remaining croissant cubes over the jam and scatter with the remaining ½ cup of blueberries. Dollop the remaining ½ cup jam by the tablespoon over the surface of the pudding.

4. Place the pudding dish inside a roasting pan and pour half of the custard over the dish. Let stand for 15 minutes, pressing occasionally to submerge the croissants.

5. Position a rack in the center of your oven and preheat the oven to 350°F.

6. Slowly pour the remaining half of the custard over the pudding dish.

7. Transfer the pudding to the oven. Pour hot but not boiling water into the roasting pan to reach halfway up the sides of the baking dish. Bake the pudding until the center still jiggles a bit but the surface is nicely browned and caramelized, 45 to 60 minutes. Remove the pudding from the water bath and let it cool for 30 minutes before serving warm. Store any leftovers in the fridge; it will keep well for 1 week.

Flourless Chocolate and Pear Spoon Cake

Serves 8

Unsalted butter, for greasing

10 ounces (283g) 72% cacao chocolate, chopped

¼ cup plus 2 tablespoons (44g) Dutch cocoa powder

½ cup (118ml) heavy cream

4 large whole eggs plus 4 large egg whites

Pinch kosher salt

1¼ cups (250g) sugar

2 ripe but firm pears, peeled, cored, and sliced ⅛ inch thick

1 recipe Crème Anglaise (page 245)

note: I love to serve this cake warm in big scoops (hence the name), but this flourless cake can be made in a 9-inch parchment-lined cake pan and sliced if you desire a cleaner presentation. In that case, cool the cake completely on a wire rack before unmolding it from the pan and removing the paper. Either way, this cake is all about setup. Having the different components ready for you before you bring the batter together is crucial.

I am not usually a fan of mixing chocolate and fruit together in baking. There are always exceptions, though, and this cake is one of them. The flourless cake is deadly chocolatey, and the pears make it slightly more balanced.

1. Position a rack in the center of your oven and preheat the oven to 300°F. Butter a 2-quart oval baking dish.

2. Combine the chocolate and cocoa powder in a heatproof bowl.

3. In a small saucepan over medium heat, warm the heavy cream until steam rises from the surface and it is hot to the touch but not yet simmering, about 5 minutes. Pour the cream over the chocolate and cocoa powder and cover the bowl with a lid or plastic wrap; set aside.

4. In the bowl of an electric mixer fitted with the whisk attachment, combine the egg whites with the salt. Beat on medium speed until frothy. With the motor running, slowly sprinkle in ¾ cup of the sugar. Once you have added all the sugar, increase the speed to medium-high and continue to beat until soft, silky peaks form, about 3 minutes. Set aside.

5. Combine the whole eggs and the remaining ½ cup sugar in a large mixing bowl and beat with a whisk until light and creamy looking; you can use an electric mixer for this step if you want.

6. Uncover the chocolate mixture and whisk the chocolate and cream until no streaks of cream or unmelted chocolate chunks remain. If needed, rewarm the chocolate in the microwave at 30-second intervals, stirring well in between each interval, to melt any chocolate chunks.

7. Fold the chocolate into the whole-egg mixture until no streaks of egg remain. Fold in the egg whites in three additions, incorporating the egg whites until the batter is smooth and consistently chocolatey.

8. Pour the batter into the prepared dish and gently tap the pan on the counter twice to dislodge any air bubbles. Smooth the top of the batter with an offset spatula and gently fan the sliced pears over the whole cake.

9. Bake the cake without opening the oven door for 30 minutes. Then rotate the cake and continue to bake about 30 minutes more, until the sides of the cake have risen up and begun to crack, and the center of the cake is set but remains a little jiggly. Turn the oven off and crack the door open. Let the cake rest in the oven for 20 minutes before serving it. Serve a scoop of the warm cake with a generous pour of cold crème anglaise.

Baked Vanilla Custard with Berries

Serves 6

berries

½ cup (83g) hulled, quartered fresh strawberries

½ cup (69g) pitted fresh cherries

2 tablespoons sugar

custard

¾ cup (150g) sugar

6 large egg yolks

½ cup (112g) mascarpone cheese, at room temperature

1¾ cups (413ml) heavy cream

1 teaspoon vanilla bean paste or extract

I first made this recipe because the idea of baked vanilla custard gave me tingles. It's such a luxurious-sounding dessert. I adore a rustic scoop of pudding for dessert and I have found that simple presentations like these always get devoured completely at dinner parties. You could serve this custard with a plate of cookies or ladyfingers for textural contrast.

1. Position a rack in the center of your oven and preheat the oven to 350°F. Have a 2-quart oval baking dish and a roasting pan large enough to hold the baking dish ready.

2. **Prepare the berries:** Combine the strawberries, cherries, and sugar in a small saucepan. Cook over medium heat without stirring, until the fruit has softened a bit and released lots of juices, about 5 minutes. Transfer the fruit and a scant ¼ cup (59ml) of the juices to the baking dish. Discard any remaining juice.

3. **Make the custard:** Combine the sugar and egg yolks in a large mixing bowl and beat vigorously with a whisk until very light and creamy looking. Add the mascarpone and beat just until combined; set aside.

4. In the bowl of an electric mixer fitted with the whisk attachment, whisk the cream and vanilla on medium speed to soft peaks, about 3 minutes. Gently fold the cream and vanilla into the mascarpone mixture until no streaks of mascarpone mixture remain.

5. Carefully dollop the custard on top of the berries. Place the baking dish in the roasting pan and place the roasting pan in the oven. Pour hot but not boiling water into the roasting pan so it comes two-thirds of the way up the sides of the baking dish.

6. Bake for about 1 hour, until lightly golden on the surface and set in the center.

7. Remove the pudding from the roasting pan and let it cool to room temperature on a wire rack. Cover the custard and chill for 6 hours or overnight. Serve chilled.

note: This recipe requires at least 6 hours of chilling time.

Vanilla Rice Pudding with Marsala-Baked Pears

Makes 8 hearty portions

rice pudding

1 cup (197g) Arborio or other fancy short-grain rice

One 14-ounce (396g) can sweetened condensed milk

1¼ cups (296ml) heavy cream

1 teaspoon vanilla bean paste or extract

1 cinnamon stick

Butter for greasing the dish

2 tablespoons sugar

marsala-baked pears

⅓ cup (79ml) Marsala wine

2 tablespoons plus 1 teaspoon sugar

2 cinnamon sticks

2-inch piece orange peel

2-inch piece lemon peel

2 ripe but firm pears, quartered, seeded, and stemmed

For several years the San Francisco Art Institute was home to one of the best college cafés in the States. Pete's Café, on the rooftop of the school, overlooking Little Italy, was run by the café's namesake, Pete Stanwood. It was the place of many culinary discoveries for me. Pete played to his audience, and the typical college fare of bagels and cereal were on offer, but he also made vegetarian curries, leafy salads, and hearty casseroles. One day we had lentil stew with rice, the next day we had the creamiest rice pudding. This recipe is an homage to Pete's Café, because I always think of that cold day in college when I realized Pete had turned the leftover rice into dessert.

1. **Make the pudding:** Position one rack in the center of your oven and the other in the top third. Preheat the oven to 350°F.

2. Place the rice in a fine-mesh colander and rinse with cold water until the water runs clear. Set aside.

3. In a 2-quart saucepan, combine the condensed milk, heavy cream, and 2 cups (472ml) water. Add the vanilla and the cinnamon stick to the saucepan. Add the rice and bring the mixture to a boil over medium heat. Reduce the heat to a simmer and cook the rice for 7 minutes. Remove the cinnamon stick.

4. Butter a 2-quart baking dish. Transfer the rice mixture to the dish and cover with a lid or tinfoil. Bake the pudding on the center rack of your oven until the rice is tender, about 25 minutes.

5. Increase the temperature to 375°F, remove the cover from the dish, and sprinkle the surface of the pudding with the sugar. Return the pudding to the oven and bake for about 20 minutes more, until the top of the pudding is golden brown. Remove the pudding from the oven and cool it to very warm room temperature before you serve it. After raising the temperature of the oven, the pears can be baked concurrently with the rice pudding.

6. **Make the pears:** Combine the Marsala wine, sugar, cinnamon sticks, orange peel, lemon peel, and ¼ cup (59ml) water in a small saucepan and cook, stirring frequently, over medium heat until the sugar has dissolved, about 3 minutes. Place the pears in a heatproof baking dish and pour the Marsala wine mixture over the fruit.

recipe continues

7. Bake the pears on the top rack of the oven, above the pudding, after raising the temperature to 375°F. After 15 minutes, carefully turn the pear quarters over and then return them to the oven. Continue to bake until the juices and wine have reduced to a thin syrup and the pears have begun to caramelize, about 20 minutes longer. Remove the fruit from the oven, remove and discard the cinnamon stick and citrus peels, and spoon some of the juices over the pears.

8. Serve the pudding warm with a wedge of pear and a drizzle of the pear-Marsala juices. The pudding and the pears keep well in the fridge for 1 week. You can prepare both in advance and reheat them, covered with a lid or tinfoil, in a 325°F oven until warm.

note: You can serve this pudding with any fruit. Peaches and fresh figs are great substitutes, but every year I look forward to serving it with pears because they ring in the cooler months, and a warm, creamy pudding is perfect on a cold night.

Passion Fruit Posset

....

*Makes 6 individual
cups of pudding*

....

½ cup (159ml) ripe passion fruit juice
    and pulp

1 cup (200g) sugar

1 teaspoon vanilla bean paste or extract

3 cups (708ml) heavy cream

¼ cup (59ml) fresh lemon juice

Freshly whipped cream, for topping
    (optional)

note: Passion fruits can sometimes be
hard to find in your local grocery store. If
you have trouble finding them there and
can't find them at a farmer's market, I
suggest visiting an Asian or Latin grocery
store to find fresh imported passion fruits
or frozen nectar. You can substitute the
fresh pulp and juice for nectar in equal
measure.

    This recipe requires at least 6 hours of
chilling time.

When my husband, Blaine, and I planned our garden, I made a list of fruit trees and vines that I needed to support my fruit-hoarding habit. Passion fruit was on the top of that list, and I sang its praises to him—"It's good for shade! It's great for privacy!"—until he made space in our garden for a couple of vines. When the season hits, most days we eat the fruits, seeds and all, scooped into a cup of yogurt (which is how Blaine first enjoyed passion fruit on a trip to Australia). Our vines are good producers, and we often have more than we can eat for breakfast, so I make it into dessert.

A posset is a simple pudding made by cooking cream with an acidic juice, such as lemon or lime, and sugar. The process is sort of like curdling the cream, but it's not separated and chunky looking. Instead the result is a smooth, creamy pudding with bright flavor.

1. Scoop the pulp and seeds from the passion fruits into a small saucepan. Cook over medium heat just until they simmer. Transfer the pulp and seeds to a blender and pulse several times to loosen the seeds from the pulp. Pour the blended passion fruit through a fine-mesh strainer set over a bowl and press out every last drop of juice.

2. Discard the seeds. Reserve 3 tablespoons of the juice for the posset, then return the rest of the juice to the saucepan. Add ¼ cup of the sugar and the vanilla. Cook over medium heat, stirring frequently. Bring the mixture to a boil, then reduce the heat to low and let simmer for 2 minutes. Remove the juice from the heat and divide it among 6 custard cups.

3. Combine the remaining ¾ cup sugar and the cream in a medium saucepan and bring to a boil over medium heat, stirring until the sugar dissolves. Reduce the heat to medium-low and let the cream and sugar simmer for 4 minutes, stirring frequently. Remove the cream from the heat and whisk in the lemon juice and the reserved passion-fruit juice. Strain the mixture and divide among the custard cups. Cool at room temperature for 30 minutes. Cover with plastic wrap and chill at least 6 hours or up to 1 week. Serve with whipped cream, if desired.

Sweet Corn Pudding with Blackberries

Makes 6 individual cups of pudding

pudding

1 tablespoon cornstarch

3 cups fresh, uncooked yellow corn kernels (4 ears of corn)

2 cups (472ml) heavy cream

¼ cup (59ml) honey

Pinch kosher salt

blackberries

2 cups (220g) fresh ripe blackberries

¼ cup (50g) sugar

One day I came into the kitchen and found my pastry cooks gazing, confused, into a container of yellow cream. They had infused some sweet cream with fresh corn and pureed it. Intending to use it to glaze doughnuts the next morning, they put the corn-infused cream in the fridge overnight, not realizing they were onto something completely different than they had expected. Pureeing the kernels into the cream released all the delicious starch and sugar from the corn, and created a fresh pudding of sorts. That's how we came up with this recipe, a very simple corn pudding with minimal ingredients and loads of natural sweetness.

1. Make the pudding: In a small bowl, combine the cornstarch with 1 tablespoon of water. Set aside.

2. Combine the corn, cream, honey, and salt in a medium saucepan and bring to a boil over medium heat. Add the cornstarch mixture to the pan (stir it up if the cornstarch has settled). Reduce the heat to low and let simmer for 1 minute. Cool the mixture to a warm room temperature.

3. Transfer the mixture to a blender and puree the corn until very smooth. Divide the puree among 6 custard cups. Cover the cups with plastic wrap and refrigerate for 6 hours or overnight.

4. Prepare the blackberries: Add the blackberries and sugar to a small saucepan over medium heat and cook, stirring, until the sugar has dissolved. Remove the berries from the heat and cool to room temperature. Store the cooked berries in the fridge until ready to use.

5. When you are ready to serve the puddings, top each one with a generous spoonful of the berries and their juices. The corn pudding and the blackberries can be made up to 1 week in advance and kept in the fridge separately until ready to use.

note: This is easily made vegan by using coconut cream in place of heavy cream. You can also make this pudding refined sugar–free by substituting honey and 1 tablespoon of water for the granulated sugar in the berries. Many different fruits would taste great here—fresh, uncooked peaches are a surprisingly delicious combination with the corn and honey flavors. Just adjust the amount of sugar you add to the fruit according to the ripeness and sweetness of the fruit you're using.

This recipe requires at least 6 hours of chilling time.

Summer Pudding

Serves 8

2½ cups (313g) fresh raspberries

2 cups (225g) fresh blackberries

1 cup (100g) fresh blueberries

1 cup (200g) sugar

2 tablespoons apricot or pear brandy

1 pound (453g) fresh strawberries,
   hulled and quartered

2-inch piece orange peel

1 medium (400g) white bread loaf,
   such as brioche or milk bread, crusts
   removed and sliced about ⅓ inch thick

Edible flowers and leaves of lemon
   verbena, for decoration (optional)

Freshly whipped cream, for serving
   (optional)

I challenge you to find a more dramatic, striking dish than a classic summer pudding. The saturated slices of white bread encasing the fruit, soaked in the vivid juices of ripe berries, have always reminded me of a can of pure magenta paint tipping over onto a white drop cloth. It's also another way to turn leftover bread and bruised ripe fruit into an impressive dessert.

1. Combine the raspberries, blackberries, and blueberries in a large saucepan over medium heat. Add the sugar and brandy and bring the berries to a gentle simmer. Add the strawberries and orange peel and reduce the heat to low. Continue cooking the fruit for 2 minutes more, just until softened but still intact. Drain the berries through a fine-mesh strainer set over a medium heatproof bowl, capturing the juices. Discard the orange peel and set the berries aside.

2. Line a 2-quart high-sided glass bowl or gelatin mold with plastic wrap, leaving a 4-inch overhang around the edges of the dish.

3. Dip the bread slices in the berry juice and line the bowl with the soaked slices of bread, cutting some slices in half or diagonally to fit the shape of the bowl.

4. Fill the soaked bread–lined bowl with the cooked berries. Top the berries with more juice-dipped bread slices. Wrap the surface of the pudding with the plastic wrap overhang. Place a plate on the surface of the covered pudding and set a soup can on top of the plate to weigh it down.

5. Chill the pudding for at least 8 hours or overnight. When you are ready to serve, unwrap the plastic from the surface of the pudding and invert onto a cake platter. Gently remove the plastic film from the pudding, decorate with edible flowers and lemon verbena leaves, if using, and serve slices with a generous scoop of whipped cream, if desired.

note: This recipe requires at least 8 hours of chilling time.

Tomato Pudding

Serves 8

½ recipe Ricotta Biscuits dough (page 242)

2 pounds (906g) ripe red tomatoes, stemmed and sliced ¾ inch thick

½ cup (100g) sugar

2 tablespoons fresh lemon juice

1 teaspoon sherry vinegar

¼ teaspoon ground nutmeg

2 tablespoons all-purpose flour

Pinch kosher salt

1 stick (113g) salted butter, room temperature

2 tablespoons heavy cream

When the tomatoes cascade like jewels on the vine, and the sun releases their sticky aroma that perfumes the garden, it's easy to be swept away and forget that all those beautiful rubies are ripening NOW and holy crap they need to be eaten or given up to the birds right NOW. You make sauce, stuff them into thick sandwiches, and eat all the salads you can, but have you ever made them into pudding? Served them for dessert, cuddled up underneath fluffy ricotta biscuits, lightly sweetened but riding that sweet/salty line like a tightrope walker? No? Well, get going!

1. Prepare the dough for the ricotta biscuits just before you are ready to make the pudding. Make the recipe as directed, and after rolling the dough out, cut it into 2-inch squares or use a round 2-inch cutter to make mini-biscuits.

2. Position a rack in the center of your oven and preheat the oven to 350°F. Place a parchment-lined baking sheet on the lower rack of the oven to catch any drips.

3. Combine the tomato slices, sugar, lemon juice, vinegar, nutmeg, flour, and salt in a 2-quart baking dish. Let the tomatoes macerate for 10 minutes.

4. Dot the tomatoes with the butter and arrange the biscuit dough on top. Brush the biscuits with the heavy cream. Bake the pudding until the biscuits are browned and baked through and the juices from the tomatoes bubble up around the edges of the dish, about 45 minutes. Serve the pudding warm. Any leftovers will keep well at room temperature overnight, but it's really best eaten the same day.

Pear and Ginger Strudel

Makes 1 strudel,
about 35 inches long,
or 12 servings

....

strudel dough

1 cup plus 2 tablespoons (141g)
    all-purpose flour, plus more for rolling

3 tablespoons melted unsalted butter,
    plus more for greasing

to assemble

1 stick (113g) unsalted butter, melted

½ cup (100g) sugar, plus more for
    sprinkling

½ cup (85g) candied ginger, chopped

½ teaspoon ground cinnamon

¼ teaspoon kosher salt

2 pounds (905g) firm pears, cored and
    sliced ¼ inch thick

¼ cup (21g) crushed ginger cookie
    crumbs

Crème fraiche, for serving (optional)

Making strudel is a kind of meditation for me. It takes a very focused and calm energy to avoid tearing it to shreds. I appreciate the delicate finished pastry in contrast to the strength of the glutinous dough that stretches so far, sometimes the length and width of the dinner table, before it gets rolled up and baked. It's an old-school recipe that traditionally calls for old bread crumbs or leftover dry cake crumbs, which reinforces the notion that nothing should be wasted and that anything can be made into dessert. I like to use leftover cookie crumbs for extra sweetness and spice.

. . . .

1. **Make the strudel dough:** Combine the flour, melted butter, and ⅓ cup (79ml) warm water in a medium bowl. Mix with your hands until a sticky ball of dough forms. Turn the dough out onto a lightly floured surface and knead it until a smooth and soft ball of dough forms, about 2 minutes. Wrap the dough in plastic and let it rest at room temperature for 2 hours.

2. **Stretch and prepare the dough:** Butter a 13 x 18-inch rimmed baking sheet and set aside.

3. Lay a clean bedsheet or extra-large kitchen towel over a table. Lightly dust the cloth with flour and place the ball of dough in the center. Dust the top of the dough with flour and use a rolling pin to roll it out into a large circle, about 12 inches in diameter. The dough will be very soft after resting, so be gentle with it.

4. To use two people to stretch the dough, stand opposite your partner on different sides of the table and work together to expand the circle of dough from the center outward. Begin by each flouring your hands. Place your hands, palms facing down, underneath the circle of dough. Each of you carefully drag your hands toward your body. The dough will begin to stretch when you do this.

5. Continue stretching the dough, always starting from the center and pulling outward, slowly extending the dough to the four corners of your work surface. Reflour your hands as necessary. Work carefully but swiftly, as the dough can start to dry and then tear. Pay special attention to the edges of the dough as you start to get a larger sheet forming; the edges will be thicker, but they can be teased with your knuckles to stretch a little bit thinner.

recipe continues

note: I recommend having a partner help you stretch the dough when you are learning how to handle it, but once you have a knack for the stretch, you can make it on your own. You can substitute different fruits, but don't fill it with anything too wet, or you run the risk of a soggy pastry instead of a shattering flake-fest.

If you are making strudel alone, you can use the rolling pin as an anchor to get the sheet of dough started. Pull the strudel dough with the backs of your hands from the rolling pin toward your body. Reposition the rolling pin and move the sheet to allow you to get at the other side of the dough. It takes a little bit of dancing around, but it is possible.

This recipe requires the dough to rest for 2 hours.

6. If you rip the dough, stretch the edge of the rip over the tear and press with your fingertips to seal up the dough again.

7. You want to stretch the dough into a 20 x 40-inch rectangle as thin as parchment.

8. **Assemble the strudel:** Position a rack in the center of your oven and preheat the oven to 400°F. When the dough is stretched, brush the entire surface with ¼ cup melted butter immediately. Use a paring knife to trim ¼ inch off the edges. This will get rid of any dough that might bake chewy once it's been rolled up inside the strudel.

9. In a small mixing bowl, combine the sugar, chopped ginger, cinnamon, and salt.

10. Combine the pears and the sugar mixture. Scatter the cookie crumbs lengthwise on half the surface of the dough. Starting 5 inches in from the edge of a long side of the dough, arrange the pears in a long pile spanning the length of the dough, leaving about 3 inches of dough at each end. Lift the 5 inches of edge along the long side of the dough and drape it over the filling. It may need to be gently stretched to cover the pears.

11. Lift the cloth on the long side and pull it up to nudge the dough to roll over, then gather the cloth and pull it toward you. Repeat. When you have a log, close off each end of the log by gathering the excess dough at the ends and twisting them like the ends of a candy wrapper. Trim off the fringe of the twist.

12. Transfer the log to the prepared baking sheet and curve it into a horseshoe shape. Brush the strudel with the remaining melted butter and sprinkle with sugar. Bake for 45 minutes, or until the strudel is deep golden brown. Remove the strudel from the oven and cool it for about 15 minutes on a wire rack. Serve warm with a dollop of crème fraiche, if desired. Strudel is best eaten the same day, while it's still crispy and warm.

Apple Brown Betty

Serves 8

8 slices brioche bread, cut into
    1-inch cubes

1 stick (113g) unsalted butter, melted

½ cup (100g) granulated sugar

3 pounds (1269g) tart apples, such as
    Pink Lady or Granny Smith, peeled,
    cored, and sliced ½ inch thick

1 cup (200g) packed dark brown sugar

3 tablespoons rose water

3 tablespoons heavy cream

2 tablespoons fresh lemon juice

2 tablespoons all-purpose flour

1 tablespoon apple cider vinegar

1 teaspoon ground cinnamon

½ teaspoon ground nutmeg

Generous pinch kosher salt

A betty is yet another vintage recipe that makes use of leftover bread and spins it into dessert. Some older recipes call for bread crumbs as the topping, but I prefer to use sweet brioche croutons for a more textural appearance and mouthfeel. The seasoning on the apples is inspired by my baker-boss lady friend Cheryl Day, who shared with me that rose water appeared in one of the first written apple pie recipes on record.

1. Position a rack in the center of your oven and preheat the oven to 350°F.

2. Lay the bread cubes on a baking sheet and toast them for 15 minutes, until they are lightly browned. Transfer the toasted bread to a heatproof bowl. Leave the oven on.

3. Pour the melted butter over the toasted cubes and toss together. Sprinkle with the granulated sugar and toss to coat. Set aside.

4. Combine the apple slices, brown sugar, rose water, heavy cream, lemon juice, flour, vinegar, cinnamon, nutmeg, and salt in a 2-quart heatproof casserole dish.

5. Arrange the bread cubes on top of the apples and bake until the juices have begun to bubble and the bread cubes are caramelized, about 1 hour. Serve warm.

note: You can make this with any fruit you'd like. It's versatile, like a crisp, crumble, or cobbler. Store-bought brioche can be substituted. I've even used cubed-up brioche hamburger buns for this recipe.

Almond and Berry Cobbler

Serves 8

1 recipe Almond Cream (page 247)

2 pounds (906g) fresh ripe berries, hulled

1½ cups (300g) sugar

2 tablespoons fresh lemon juice

2 tablespoons all-purpose flour

Pinch kosher salt

In some parts of the baking world, the recipe for Peach and Ricotta Biscuit Cobbler (page 122) would not pass as a cobbler. The biscuit topping is too fancy and substantial for it to meet the definition. For those looking for something closer to a Texas-style cobbler (where a cakey batter replaces the biscuits), I offer this not-so-standard but pretty-dang-close version made with almond cream instead of the traditional cake batter or biscuit topping.

1. If the almond cream was made in advance, take it out of the fridge and let it sit on the counter until it is a soft, scoopable texture.

2. Position a rack in the center of your oven and preheat the oven to 350°F. Place a parchment-lined baking sheet on the lower rack of the oven to catch any drips.

3. Combine the berries, sugar, lemon juice, flour, and salt in a 2-quart baking dish. Drop the almond cream on top of the fruit in generous spoonfuls, leaving some space between each scoop.

4. Bake the cobbler until the almond cream has browned and puffed up and the juices bubble vigorously around the edges of the dish, about 45 minutes. Serve the cobbler warm. Any leftovers will keep well at room temperature overnight, but it's really best eaten the same day.

Peach and Ricotta Biscuit Cobbler

Serves 8

2 pounds (908g) ripe peaches, skinned, pitted, and cut into ¾-inch pieces (about 6 cups)

1½ cups (300g) sugar

2 tablespoons fresh lemon juice

2 tablespoons all-purpose flour

1 teaspoon ground cinnamon

Pinch kosher salt

½ recipe Ricotta Biscuits dough (page 242), cut into 2-inch squares

2 tablespoons heavy cream, for brushing

Because I love biscuits, I have always preferred true cobblers over crisps and crumbles. A cobbler delivers that doughy-dumpling texture where the biscuits meet the fruit juices and braises. I find that on most dessert menus there is a cobbler listed and that it is almost always a crisp. You can look at page 127 for a description of a crisp and see why the distinction is necessary. But both desserts make great use of a bounty of fruit and can be served at pretty much any meal. In terms of cobblers, for me peach cobbler is the only cobbler, but of course you can use any fruit you like in equal measure.

1. Position a rack in the center of your oven and preheat the oven to 350°F. Place a parchment-lined baking sheet on the lower rack of the oven to catch any drips.

2. Combine the peaches, sugar, lemon juice, flour, cinnamon, and salt in a 2-quart baking dish. Arrange the biscuits on top of the filling and brush the surface with the heavy cream.

3. Bake the cobbler until the biscuits are browned and baked through and the juices bubble vigorously around the edges of the dish, about 45 minutes. Serve the cobbler warm. Any leftovers will keep well at room temperature overnight, but it's really best eaten the same day.

Peaches

There have been times in my life when a piece of fruit has saved me. I know this sounds overly dramatic. "Woman Saved by Peach" seems implausible. But there was a day not too long ago when I ate a peach that made the hair on the back of my neck stand up and tears come to my eyes, breaking open the knot of anxiety and stress that had formed inside me from a very hard day at work. It started before I had even put the slice into my mouth, when the knife broke the skin of a gorgeous July Flame peach and a trickle of garnet-colored juice dripped down onto the table. I had the beauty of an entire season right there in my hand, and it was delicious. I felt a knot inside myself begin to loosen.

What did I do after that soul-opening moment? I dried the tears that had begun to well, gobbled up the perfect peach, and feverishly wrote down six recipe ideas that I hoped would do that peach justice. Cooking a peach well is a heavy burden because a perfect peach should be eaten and savored and worshiped as is. Much later I would leave my position at the restaurant I worked at, and look back on that time with the peach as being the marker for the moment I knew it was time to move on.

I have had some very poetic moments with fruit growers, and it leads me to think that the particular soul of each farmer draws them to grow a specific crop. David "Mas" Masumoto, the famous peach farmer known all across the Bay Area of California and beyond, is a good example. I once watched him tenderly cut a half-fallen branch from a nectarine tree, snapped under the weight of so much heavy fruit, and pass the branch to my nephew. He put his arm around my nephew's shoulders and said, "Look, it's like he is cradling a newborn, they're babies . . ." With an open smile and a laugh, he continued on through the orchard like a shepherd, greeting every guest on the farm that day with a calmness and kindness.

Every year, I bring one perfect peach to my therapist and one to my best friend because it's important to share things that are beautiful, especially with those who will consider the beauty and sit with it for a moment. I like to force a peach on a stranger who has spotted them on my farmer's market cart—"Here, take it. It's perfect. You should try it."—hoping to inspire them to take a moment to consider the fruit and the perfect fragility of a peach, but also to carry forward the spirit and generosity of the wonderful farmers like Mas and his family who share their painstaking tending of the land with us.

Fruit Crisp or Crumble but Not Cobbler

Serves 8

This is not a cobbler. If you want a cobbler, please see page 122. This is a rubric for making crisps and crumbles, those delightful and simple desserts (or breakfasts!) that you can throw together in an hour and a half. The basic architecture of a crisp/crumble is a casserole dish filled with seasoned fruit, and topped with an unleavened mixture of flour, grains, and possibly nuts that have been crumbled together with sugar and fat. Bake that and you'll have a crisp, I mean crumble! With almost endless possibilities for any season, making a crisp is really as easy as knowing the parameters of the humble casserole dessert.

For the fruit, you want to choose ripe and juicy. It's a great way to use up bruised or broken fruit. The amount and type of sweetener and spices you use depend on your preferences and the fruit you're using. Pears with maple syrup and cardamom is a wonderful fall combination. Nectarines with lemon verbena and honey is divine. Apricots with almond extract, rose water, and brown sugar tastes exotic. The important thing to remember is to sample the fruit before you bake it and decide how much sweetener and spice to use. Too little, and you may be left without a sauce. Too much, and you might miss the fruit flavor altogether.

Here is a good place to start:

2 pounds (906g) fruit of your choice

½ cup (or less depending on sweetness of fruit) sweetener, such as honey, brown sugar, granulated sugar, or maple syrup

1 to 2 tablespoons flour or cornstarch (less for average ripe fruit and more for very juicy, ripe fruit)

Spices, edible flowers, leaves, or extracts, such as cinnamon, vanilla, nutmeg, saffron, rose, lemon verbena, thyme, ginger, or cardamom

For the crisp or crumble topping, the recipe is just as flexible. You can combine any number of flours, grains, fats, and other add-ins to make your topping. The ingredients in the topping often make their way down into the fruit and sometimes aid

recipe continues

in thickening the juices. The fat in the crumble helps to create a velvety sauce with the fruit juices. As a guide, I suggest the following measurements:

2 cups all-purpose flour, old-fashioned rolled oats, fine-ground cornmeal, or wheat bran (or combination)

½ cup chopped nuts of your choice

1 cup unsalted butter, browned butter, olive oil, coconut oil, or lard (room temperature)

½ cup white granulated or packed dark brown sugar (or alternative sweetener like coconut sugar)

1 teaspoon kosher salt

. . . .

1. Position a rack in the center of your oven and preheat the oven to 350°F. Place a parchment-lined baking sheet on the lower rack of the oven to catch any drips.

2. If you are using large fruits, cut the fruits into smaller chunks or wedges. Remove the cores on apples and pears, if using, but peeling is optional (I never peel them for a simple dish like this). If you're using berries, use them whole, or maybe cut extra-large strawberries in half.

3. Taste the fruit and decide on your direction. Combine the fruit with the sweetener, thickening agent, and flavorings of your choice. You can mix all of this together in the actual dish you are going to bake in. I use a round 2-quart Pyrex dish with a matching lid (helpful for storing leftovers or bringing the crisp to a party).

4. In a separate bowl, combine the flour and/or grains with the nuts, fat, sugar, and salt. Use a large spoon to incorporate the fat into the dry ingredients until you have something resembling the crashed remains of a sand castle on the beach.

5. Cover the fruit with the topping. Here is one of my only rules for this dessert: Do not smash or pack the topping down. The topping will settle in during baking, and I prefer a topping with a craggy-looking surface and an open structure to allow the fruit and juices to peek through the surface.

6. Bake the crisp until the topping is browned and the juices bubble enthusiastically at the edges, about 45 minutes. (That's the second rule: Bake the crisp until the juices really flow and bubble.)

7. Serve the crisp or crumble (not a cobbler!) warm. It keeps well at room temperature for 1 day. Store any leftovers in the fridge for up to 1 week.

Rhubarb and Blood Orange Pavlova

....

Makes one 9-inch round pavlova

....

meringue

4 large egg whites, room temperature

1 cup (200g) sugar

1 teaspoon cornstarch

½ teaspoon apple cider vinegar

¼ teaspoon kosher salt

1 cup (100g) unsweetened shredded coconut

to assemble

2 cups (472ml) heavy cream

1 recipe Slow-Cooked Rhubarb (page 208)

3 blood oranges, segments only

Sometimes, even after all the years we have spent together, I am shocked by my husband's opinions on desserts. He will turn away a fruit-filled slice of pie and he never finishes a piece of chocolate cake, but he will CRUSH an entire pavlova if left alone with it. It is one of his favorite desserts because it is textural, fresh, creamy, and tart. It ticks all the boxes for memorable sweet moments, and it's impressive in an effortless and messy way.

....

1. **Make the meringue:** Position a rack in the center of your oven and preheat the oven to 250°F. Line a baking sheet with parchment paper.

2. In the bowl of an electric mixer fitted with the whisk attachment, beat the egg whites on medium-high speed until stiff peaks form, about 3 minutes. With the mixer running on medium speed, slowly rain in the sugar about 1 tablespoon at a time. It may seem like an arduous task to add the sugar in at such a slow pace, but this intentional act allows time for the sugar to dissolve into the egg whites, giving the meringue an even structure. Once all the sugar is in, add the cornstarch, vinegar, and salt and increase the speed to medium-high. Beat until silky stiff peaks form, about 5 minutes more.

3. Spoon the meringue onto the prepared baking sheet and use a spatula to shape it into a rustic circle about 9 inches across. Use the back of a spoon to pull the edge of the circle up in swoops, creating an outer rim of meringue. Sprinkle the edge of the meringue with ½ cup of the coconut.

4. Bake for 1 hour, or until firm and dry to the touch. Turn off the oven and prop the door open (you can use a wooden spoon if need be). Allow the pavlova to cool completely in the oven, about 1 hour.

5. **Assemble the pavlova:** In the bowl of an electric mixer fitted with the whisk attachment, beat the cream on medium speed until you have smooth, soft peaks, about 2 minutes. Remove the bowl from the machine and manually whisk the cream 2 or 3 more times to create pronounced peaks.

recipe continues

note: You can substitute any combination of fruit, although I always use a cooked fruit and a fresh fruit. Lemon or passion fruit curd are excellent additions to a pavlova. Of course I prefer using a homemade curd such as the lemon curd on page 212, but using a store-bought curd is a great way to save some time.

6. Lay the meringue base on a large cake plate. Scoop three-quarters of the whipped cream on top of the meringue and spread it around with the back of a spoon. Arrange half the cooked rhubarb and blood orange segments all over the cream. Dollop the remaining whipped cream on top and add the rest of the fruit. Sprinkle the pavlova with the remaining ½ cup coconut.

7. This dessert is best served chilled and eaten the same day, but it can be prepared a few hours in advance and kept in the fridge. Alternately you can prepare each element of the pavlova and store them separately up to 1 day in advance.

Pies, Tarts, and Galettes

Sour Apple Pie

Apple Crumb Slab Pie

Banana Cream Pie

Berry Buttermilk Pie

Black and Blue Pie
with Brown Sugar Crumb

July Flame Peach Pie

Boysenberry Hand Pies

Sweet 100 Turnovers

Rhubarb Pie

Frankie's Lemon Pie

Pear and Cranberry Pie

Honey-Glazed Strawberry Pie

The Lime Pie That Saved Us

Boiled Maple "Pumpkin" Pie

Caramelized Pineapple Tarts

Rhubarb Tarte Tatin

Prune and Pistachio Cream Tart

Strawberry Galettes

Apricot Galette

Provençal-Style Cheesecake

Make a Nice Pie

The pie recipes (and all the other recipes) in this book received extensive testing and scrutiny. The art of good pie is a balancing act of variables. In my kitchen, most of the fillings for fruit pies are made by taste and not by strict measurements. Since you are not baking next to me, I have tried my best to describe all the intuitive stuff that makes good pie.

Fruits come in varying degrees of ripeness, and recipes need to be adjusted to manage fluctuations in juices, sweetness, and firmness. If you are already a skilled pie maker, you will have learned this art of managing fruit. For novice pie makers, I have included a few tips and solutions in How to Choose Fruit (page 13).

Since there are so many variables at play when you are baking an all-fruit pie, time and temperature become ingredients. Structure also plays a role. The open structure of a lattice top allows steam to evaporate more freely than a vented solid crust; a crumble top releases extra thickener into the filling, so adjustments should be made to the amount of thickener in the fruit.

In my daily baking life, I don't make a lot of lattice-topped pies. I prefer the rustic hilltops of a full crust marked with the primitive language of the baker. My sous chef Krystle adores lattice crusts and makes the prettiest variations on the weave I've ever seen.

If you are making a pie to impress people, a lattice top always wins in the looks department: for instance, a wedding pie with a lattice can symbolize the weaving together of families. (If we are making a pie for a wedding, we always include a braided lattice to drive that sentiment home.) But a lattice isn't always practical due to the unruly nature of cutting into a lattice. If your filling is not completely set, the strips of the lattice will move and break and the slice will look messy. In my kitchen, the lattice spacing is always set very close so that it fuses together to form a complete crust but also maintains a little of that open-structure look.

I prefer taste over beauty every day, and a fruit filling with too much thickener does not taste good. I aim for a softly set fruit filling with just the right amount of thickened juices and fruit so that the slice can stand on its own but also oozes a pleasing amount of silky sauce. That is how my recipes are designed, to use ripe fruit that is just barely held together with enough starch to form a lightly thickened sauce on the plate. Starch thickens as it cools, which is important to remember if you plan to serve the pie warm from the oven. That warm, oozing pie will be settled and a little stiffer the next day.

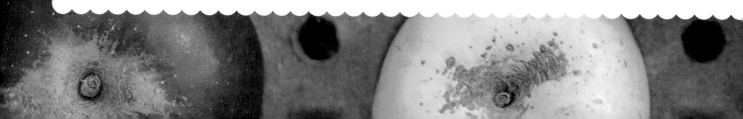

All pie makers should develop their own personal finishing style; it is your signature. Years ago I met a woman in Arizona who prepared a hundred pies for a diner once a week. She kept the unbaked pies in a large chest freezer, each one marked with her own language of cuts for identification. She made a really great rhubarb pie with just rhubarb, sugar, and lemon. Each pie in that freezer was evidence of a lifetime of practice. The practice is an ingredient, too.

I advocate for the use of glass pie dishes, especially for beginning pie makers, as they allow for the visual references for doneness to be obvious. The bottom of the pie should be golden brown, same as the top, but sometimes those things do not happen at the same time. The top crust should be deeply bronzed. If your bottom crust needs to catch up to the top, tent the pie with tinfoil and continue baking until the bottom crust glows with color. A fully baked bottom crust is so important to the taste and structure of a pie: Unbaked/pasty/soggy bottom pies are a sad experience and totally avoidable!

I preheat the oven to a high temperature of 400°F to blast the crust with heat at the beginning. Through trial and error, and many different ovens, I have found that it's the best way for me to make sure my crust stays in the shape I want it to. I lower the temperature as soon as the pie goes into the oven to prevent the high temperature from cooking the top crust too quickly.

Some pies call for a single crust, and they are in two categories: par-baked and fully baked. The former is used for recipes where the filling is a custard of some kind. The baking time of a custard pie is much shorter than a fresh-fruit pie, and so the crust is baked halfway before you fill it and then baked again until the custard has set. Fully baked single crusts are used for fresh pudding or fruit fillings that will not be baked and are usually chilled before serving.

In both cases, the crust is lined with tinfoil or parchment paper and filled with either beans or pie weights to prevent the crust from bubbling up and shifting during baking. I use beans; they are cheap and can be composted after a few uses.

To bake the nicest fruit pie you can whip up, fresh fruit is always best. You can make a great pie from frozen fruit as well; it just takes a little more work. Freezing fruit softens the structure a lot, and once the fruit is thawed, the water escapes the fruit more easily. If you do not treat it correctly, this can make a soupy pie. Frozen peaches, apples, and rhubarb are all suitable to be baked without thawing and draining.

Frozen blueberries, strawberries, and cherries must be thawed first, and for best results should be precooked with the sugar and starch until the juices are thickened. The filling can then be cooled and frozen again, or used for a tasty pie.

Raspberries and blackberries are generally okay to use straight from the freezer in small amounts, but if you were to make a pie with 100 percent blackberries and use frozen fruit, I would recommend treating the blackberries like blueberries and precooking them. If you would like to use frozen berries mixed with fresh apples, pears, or peaches, you can add them frozen to the filling without risking a wet pie.

Sour Apple Pie

....

Makes one 9½-inch pie

....

1½ pounds (680g) apples, peeled, cored, and sliced ¼ inch thick: Use a mixture of sweet/soft apples (such as McIntosh, Dorsett Golden, or Golden Delicious) and tart/firm apples (such as Cripps Pink, Granny Smith, or Mutsu)

1 recipe Slow-Cooked Sour Apples (page 207)

¾ cup (150g) packed dark brown sugar, plus more to taste

½ cup (115g) sour cream

3 tablespoons all-purpose flour, plus more for rolling

1 teaspoon kosher salt

1 recipe Flaky Butter Crust (page 234); see Note

2 tablespoons heavy cream

1 tablespoon granulated sugar

I call this "Sour Apple Pie" not because it lacks sweetness but because it has a rich apple filling that gets its "sour" from sour cream. The result is a delicious caramel apple flavor, and the addition of the sour cream creates a wonderful velvety sauce for the fruit. Using more than one variety of apple, both raw and cooked, creates a true and complex apple flavor. I've been known to use up to six different varieties in one pie. I suggest choosing two varieties of apples to start; look for one from the sweet/soft category and one from the tart/firm.

....

1. Combine the fresh apple slices, slow-cooked apples, brown sugar, sour cream, flour, and salt in a large bowl. Toss to combine, taste for sweetness, and adjust if necessary; set aside.

2. Remove the dough from the fridge and remove the plastic from each piece. If your dough has been chilled overnight, it will need to sit at room temperature a bit before rolling–this will take 10 to 15 minutes.

3. Lightly flour your work surface. Once pliable, roll the disc of dough out into a 12-inch circle. Use flour throughout the rolling process as needed to prevent sticking. Transfer the rolled dough to a 9½-inch pie dish. Trim so that 1 inch of dough hangs over the edge of the dish.

4. On the same floured surface, roll the rectangle of dough out into a 10 x 11-inch rectangle. Cut into ten 1-inch strips.

5. Position a rack in the center of your oven and preheat the oven to 400°F. Place a parchment-lined baking sheet on the lower rack to catch any juice drippings.

6. Pour the apple filling into the crust and gently press the fruit so that the apples lie flat across the surface. Pour any of the juices that may have collected in the bottom of the bowl over the apples.

7. Lay 5 strips of dough evenly over the filling. Gently fold the second and fourth strips back halfway. Lay a new strip of dough perpendicular to the other strips across the center of the pie. Unfold the 2 folded strips so they lie flat on top of the perpendicular strip. Fold back the first, third, and fifth strips. Lay a new strip of dough ½ inch away from the last one. Unfold the 3 folded strips. Fold back the second and fourth strips. Lay a new strip of dough ½ inch from the last one and unfold the 2 strips.

recipe continues

note: Make the Flaky Butter Crust 2 to 24 hours in advance so it can chill prior to you rolling it out. Shape half of the dough into a disc and the other half into a rectangle before wrapping in plastic and chilling in the fridge.

8. Repeat on the other side with the 2 remaining strips: fold back alternating strips, then lay a strip of dough on top and unfold. Alternating the strips creates a woven effect.

9. Trim the strips so that they leave a ½-inch overhang. Press the ends of the lattice flush with the bottom crust. Fold the edge of the crust under and press gently into the dish while you crimp or pinch the edge of the crust all the way around. Everyone crimps differently; my general method is to pinch a section of the dough with the thumb and forefinger of my left hand while simultaneously pushing an indentation into the center of the pinched area with the tip of my right forefinger. Just writing that made me a little dizzy, but crimping is decorative and can be customized to whatever feels right for the pie maker. A simple edge of fork indentations is also very lovely. Brush the lattice generously with the heavy cream. Sprinkle the strips of the lattice with the granulated sugar.

10. Place the whole pie in the freezer for 10 minutes.

11. Place the pie on the center rack of the oven and reduce the heat to 375°F. Bake for 1 hour, or until the crust is a deep golden brown and the juices from the pie are bubbling. Check the bottom crust to make sure it has cooked through by *carefully* lifting the pie up with pot holders so that you can get a peek at the crust underneath. If the bottom crust has not turned golden brown, return the pie to the oven and continue baking until you see color appear. If the top is done cooking well before the bottom, loosely cover the top with foil until the bottom catches up.

12. Cool the pie for 2 hours on a wire rack before serving. Store the pie covered at room temperature for 1 day and up to 1 week in the fridge.

Apple Crumb Slab Pie

Makes one 13 x 18-inch pie

1 recipe Flaky Butter Crust (page 234), undivided

All-purpose flour, for rolling

crumb topping

2 cups (250g) all-purpose flour

1 cup (200g) packed dark brown sugar

1 stick (113g) unsalted butter, melted and cooled

½ teaspoon kosher salt

filling

4 pounds (1812g) tart and firm apples, such as Granny Smith or Pink Lady, peeled, cored, and cut into ½-inch pieces

Zest and juice of 1 lemon

½ cup (100g) sugar

1 teaspoon ground cinnamon

1 teaspoon vanilla bean paste or extract

½ teaspoon kosher salt

note: Make the Flaky Butter Crust 2 to 24 hours in advance so that it can be properly chilled prior to rolling. When preparing the dough here, don't divide it—keep it as 1 piece.

Slab pie is a fun way to make pie for twenty-five people without making multiple pies. It's not a true pie ratio. It's slimmer in profile and contains less filling per inch than a round pie, but it's still pie. It's a huge pie that saves you lots of time and makes you a superhero for producing dessert for a big crowd. You will win the office potluck award with your slab pie. You will be a potluck dessert legend.

1. Position a rack in the center of your oven and preheat the oven to 400°F. Place a parchment-lined baking sheet on the lower rack to catch any juices that fall when baking the slab pie. Have a 13 x 18-inch rimmed baking sheet nearby.

2. **Make the crust:** Remove the dough from the fridge and remove the plastic from the disc. If your dough has been chilled overnight, it will need to sit at room temperature a bit before rolling—this will take 10 to 15 minutes.

3. Lightly flour your work surface and roll the pie dough into a 14 x 19-inch rectangle. Transfer the crust to the rimmed baking sheet and press into the bottom edges and up the sides. Fold the extra dough under itself and crimp or pinch decoratively. Refrigerate the crust while you prepare the topping and filling.

4. **Make the crumb topping:** Combine the flour, brown sugar, melted butter, and salt in a large bowl. Mix the butter into the flour and sugar with your hands, fluffing and squeezing the mixture until you have crumbs that look like pebbles in the sand; set aside.

5. **Make the filling:** Combine the apples, lemon zest and juice, sugar, cinnamon, vanilla, and salt in another large bowl and toss the mixture together so that all the apples are coated.

6. **Assemble the pie:** Fill the pie crust with the apple mixture and scatter the crumble on top.

7. Place the pie on the center rack of the oven and reduce the temperature to 375°F. Bake until the crust is golden brown and the juices are bubbling, about 1 hour. Let cool completely on a wire rack before serving. Leftovers can be stored in a sealed container at room temperature for 1 day or up to 1 week in the fridge.

Banana Cream Pie

. . . .

Makes one 9½-inch pie

. . . .

All-purpose flour, for rolling

½ recipe Flaky Butter Crust (page 234)

½ recipe Almond Cream (page 247)

6 to 8 medium-ripe bananas or
   12 baby bananas

1 tablespoon granulated sugar

1 recipe Pastry Cream (page 246)

1 cup (236ml) heavy whipping cream

2 tablespoons confectioners' sugar

This pie came to be after a longtime customer showed up at our kitchen door with two stalks of fresh, local bananas that he had grown in his yard in the Malibu hills. I placed the entire stalks, flowers and all, on a top shelf in the kitchen and waited patiently for the bananas to ripen. Those bananas deserved an over-the-top preparation to honor the weeks of ripening it took for them all to be ready to use. Weighing in at a staggering four pounds, this is not your average late-night-diner banana cream pie. A rich layer of almond cream and baked bananas line the crust, followed by vanilla custard piled high and fresh bananas, and then a topping of whipped cream.

. . . .

1. If your dough has been chilled overnight, it will need to sit at room temperature a bit before rolling—this will take 10 to 15 minutes. Lightly flour your work surface and roll the pie dough out to a 13-inch round that is ⅛ inch thick. Transfer to a 9½-inch pie dish and use your fingertips to relax the dough into the shape of the pie dish, leaving a 2-inch overhang around the edge of the dish. Fold the edge of the dough under itself. Use your thumb and forefinger to crimp the edge of the dough, pressing the dough into the dish and making sure the dough extends to the outer edge. This anchors the crust inside the dish, which results in a proud crown of crust after baking. Freeze the crimped crust for about 20 minutes, until the dough is very cold.

2. Position a rack in the center of your oven and preheat the oven to 375°F.

3. Line the crust with heavy-duty foil, leaving a 1½-inch overhang. Trace your fingertips over the foil overhang and gently press it into the crimp. Fill the foil-lined crust with pie weights or dried beans. Bake for 20 to 25 minutes, until the crust is golden around the edges. Remove from the oven and lift out the foil and pie weights. Leave the oven on.

4. Spread the almond cream in the bottom of the crust. Cut half of the bananas into ¼-inch-thick slices, slightly on the bias. Beginning at the sides of the pie crust, fan the slices to cover the almond cream in overlapping rows. Sprinkle the bananas with the granulated sugar. Bake for 20 minutes, or until the almond cream has puffed and the bananas have browned. Let the baked shell cool completely on a wire rack.

recipe continues

note: Prepare the Flaky Butter Crust 2 to 24 hours before starting the pie, as it needs to chill prior to rolling it out.

To achieve a clean slice with well-defined layers, the finished pie needs to chill for at least 4 hours before serving.

5. **Assemble the pie:** Spread half of the pastry cream over the baked bananas and almond cream. Cut the rest of the bananas into ¼-inch-thick slices, on the bias. Beginning at the sides of the pie crust, fan the slices of fresh banana in overlapping rows on top of the pastry cream.

6. Cover the fresh bananas with the remaining pastry cream and smooth it into an even layer. Cover the pie with plastic wrap and place it in the fridge while you make the whipped cream.

7. In the bowl of an electric mixer fitted with the whisk attachment, combine the cream and confectioners' sugar and beat until soft peaks form. Pile the whipped cream on top of the pie and swoosh it around with the back of a spoon.

8. Loosely cover with plastic wrap and refrigerate for at least 4 hours. When you are ready to serve the pie, soak a kitchen towel in hot water and fold it in half. Place the cold pie on top of the towel to release the buttery crust from the dish.

Berry Buttermilk Pie

....

Makes one 9½-inch pie

....

½ cup (63g) all-purpose flour, plus more for rolling

½ recipe Flaky Butter Crust (page 234)

2 tablespoons fine-ground yellow cornmeal

½ teaspoon kosher salt

1 cup (200g) plus 1 tablespoon sugar

1 stick plus 2 tablespoons (141g) unsalted butter, at room temperature

2 teaspoons freshly grated orange zest

1 teaspoon vanilla bean paste or extract

4 large eggs, at room temperature

1¼ cups (295ml) buttermilk, at room temperature

2 cups (300g) fresh or frozen mixed berries, such as blueberries, raspberries, and blackberries

Brimming with sweet and vibrant fruit, this is one of my favorite uses for a few handfuls of ripe farmer's market berries. It's not an expensive pie to make, unlike a whole blackberry pie. It's a conservative pie that makes use of those slightly smashed raspberries that get left in the bottom of the carton. I think the surface of a Berry Buttermilk Pie looks so appealing—the broken fruit staining the buttermilk custard, flecked with orange zest and vanilla bean—sometimes I find myself gazing at one like a child would gaze at a picture of the solar system.

....

1. If your dough has been chilled overnight, it will need to sit at room temperature a bit before rolling—this will take 10 to 15 minutes. Lightly flour your work surface and roll the pie dough out to a 13-inch round that is ⅛ inch thick. Transfer to a 9½-inch pie dish and use your fingertips to relax the dough into the shape of the pie dish, leaving a 2-inch overhang around the edge of the dish. Fold the dough under itself. Use your thumb and forefinger to crimp the edge of the dough, pressing the crimp into the pie dish and making sure the dough extends to the outer edge of the dish. This anchors the crust inside the dish, which results in a proud crown of crust after baking. Freeze the crimped crust for about 20 minutes, until the dough is very cold.

2. Position a rack in the center of your oven and preheat the oven to 375°F.

3. Line the crust with heavy-duty foil, leaving a 1½-inch overhang. Trace your fingertips over the foil overhang and gently press it into the crimp. Fill the foil-lined crust with pie weights or dried beans. Bake for 20 to 25 minutes, until the crust is golden around the edges. Remove from the oven and lift out the foil and pie weights. Cool the pie crust completely. Reduce the oven temperature to 325°F.

4. Combine the flour, cornmeal, and salt in a small bowl; set aside.

5. In the bowl of an electric mixer fitted with the paddle attachment, combine 1 cup of the sugar, the butter, orange zest, and vanilla. Beat the mixture on medium until light and fluffy, about 4 minutes. Incorporate the eggs 1 at a time, beating until well combined after each addition. Scrape down the bottom and sides of the bowl.

recipe continues

note: Make the Flaky Butter Crust
2 to 24 hours in advance so that it can be
properly chilled prior to rolling.

6. Reduce the speed to low and add the cornmeal mixture. Beat until no dry bits remain. With the motor running on low speed, gradually add the buttermilk and beat until just combined, about 1 minute. Scrape down the bottom and sides of the bowl and beat the mixture on low speed for 30 more seconds.

7. Transfer the filling to the cooled crust. If you're using fresh berries, make sure the berries are completely dry; if the berries are frozen, use them straight from the freezer—they will stay closer to the surface. Carefully arrange the berries on the surface of the filling. Don't worry if some of them sink! Sprinkle the remaining 1 tablespoon of sugar over the surface of the pie.

8. Bake until the pie filling is golden and puffed at the edges and the center wobbles slightly when touched, about 1 hour. Transfer the pie to a wire rack and let cool for at least 2 hours before slicing. Store any leftovers in the fridge; this custard is sensitive to heat after baking.

Black and Blue Pie with Brown Sugar Crumb

Makes one 9½-inch pie

for the brown sugar crumb

1 cup (120g) all-purpose flour

½ cup (45g) old-fashioned rolled oats

¼ cup (50g) packed dark brown sugar

1 teaspoon kosher salt

1 stick (113g) unsalted butter, melted

2 tablespoons whole milk

for the crust and filling

3 tablespoons all-purpose flour, plus more for rolling

½ recipe Flaky Butter Crust (page 234)

3 cups (380g) fresh huckleberries or blueberries

3 cups (330g) fresh blackberries, boysenberries, or marionberries

¾ cup (150g) granulated sugar

2 tablespoons fresh lemon juice

Generous pinch kosher salt

Very cold heavy cream, for serving (optional)

This pie is a true luxury. Since it contains about 2½ pounds of luscious berries, it's not an inexpensive pie to make. It is worth every penny, though, especially if you can get fresh huckleberries (the blue in "black and blue"). They are tart, floral, and complex with deep berry flavor.

1. **Make the brown sugar crumb:** In a medium bowl, combine the flour, oats, brown sugar, and salt in a small mixing bowl. Combine the melted butter and milk in a measuring cup and slowly pour it into the flour mixture. Use a fork or your hands to fluff the mixture until the butter is distributed throughout. Squeeze a few handfuls of the crumb mixture into large clumps. Refrigerate until ready to use.

2. **Prepare the crust:** If your dough has been chilled overnight, it will need to sit at room temperature a bit before rolling—this will take 10 to 15 minutes. Lightly flour your work surface and roll the pie dough out to a 13-inch round that is ⅛ inch thick. Transfer to a 9½-inch pie dish and use your fingertips to relax the dough into the shape of the pie dish, leaving a 2-inch overhang around the edge of the dish. Fold the extra dough under itself. Use your thumb and forefinger to crimp the edge of the dough, pressing the crimp into the pie dish and making sure the dough extends to the outer edge of the dish. This anchors the crust inside the dish, which results in a proud crown of crust after baking. Freeze the crimped crust for about 20 minutes, until the dough is very cold.

3. Position a rack in the center of your oven and preheat the oven to 400°F. Place a parchment-lined baking sheet on the lower rack to catch any juices that fall from the pie when it bakes.

4. **Make the filling:** Combine the flour, berries, granulated sugar, lemon juice, and salt in a large mixing bowl. Gently toss to coat the berries. Squeeze just one handful of berries to break them open, and stir the smashed fruit into the filling—this helps to create a sauce by introducing a small amount of the berry juices to the filling before it bakes.

5. **Assemble the pie:** Transfer the filling to the chilled crust. Top the pie with the crumble, breaking large clumps into chunks of varying sizes as you sprinkle it all over the filling. Place the pie on the center rack of the oven and reduce the heat to 375°F. Bake until the crust is a deep golden brown and the juices from the pie are bubbling, about 1 hour.

6. Remove the pie from the oven and transfer to a wire rack. Cool for at least 2 hours before serving. Store any leftovers covered in the fridge for up to 1 week.

July Flame Peach Pie

Makes one 9½-inch pie

1 recipe Flaky Butter Crust (page 234)

3 tablespoons all-purpose flour, plus more for rolling

3 pounds (1359g) ripe but firm peaches (do not use white peaches)

¾ cup (150g) granulated sugar

1½ tablespoons fresh lemon juice

1 teaspoon vanilla bean paste or extract

¼ teaspoon ground mace

2 tablespoons unsalted butter, room temperature

3 tablespoons heavy cream

1 tablespoon raw turbinado sugar

note: Make the Flaky Butter Crust 2 to 24 hours in advance, as it needs to chill before you roll it out. Make this pie with amazing nectarines instead of peaches, if those taste better—nectarines are often higher in acid and you can leave them unpeeled in the pie.

It is important to find a peach variety with high acid and sugar content, so stick to yellow peach varieties for this pie.

The interior of a ripe July Flame peach is the color of a dramatic summer sunset. Use the best, juiciest, and most vibrant peaches you can find for this pie.

1. Remove the pie dough from the fridge and remove the plastic from each disc. If your dough has been chilled overnight, it will need to sit at room temperature a bit before rolling—this will take 10 to 15 minutes. Line a baking sheet with parchment paper.

2. Lightly flour a flat work surface and roll 1 disc of the pie dough out to a 12-inch round that is ⅛ inch thick. Transfer the dough to a 9½-inch pie dish and use your fingertips to press the dough into the shape of the pie dish, leaving a 2-inch overhang around the edge of the dish. Roll the second disc of dough out to a 10-inch round and transfer it to the prepared baking sheet. Chill the bottom and top crust in the fridge until very cold, 15 to 25 minutes.

3. Wash the peaches and remove their skins using a vegetable peeler or paring knife. Cut the peaches into ¾-inch-thick slices. In a large mixing bowl, combine the peaches with the flour, granulated sugar, lemon juice, vanilla, and mace and toss to coat all the fruit in the seasoning. Let stand for 5 minutes. Remove the top and bottom crusts from the refrigerator.

4. Transfer the peaches and their juices to the chilled pie shell. Dot the fruit with the butter.

5. Gently drape the top crust over the fruit. Press the edges of the pie shell together to seal. Fold the edge of the pie dough under itself and crimp the edge of the crust with your thumb and forefinger, pressing gently into the pie dish as you crimp. Brush the top crust with the heavy cream and sprinkle with the turbinado sugar. Place the whole pie in the freezer for 15 minutes.

6. Position a rack in the center of your oven and preheat the oven to 400°F. Place a parchment-lined baking sheet on the lower rack to catch any juices that fall from the pie when it bakes.

7. Remove the pie from the freezer and cut a few slits in the top crust—this allows steam to escape from the filling while the pie bakes. Bake the pie for 30 minutes, lower the oven temperature to 375°F, and rotate the pie. Continue baking until the filling is bubbling and the crust is deeply golden brown, about 30 more minutes.

8. Cool the pie on a wire rack for 2 hours before cutting. Store at room temperature for 1 day or in the fridge for up to 1 week.

Boysenberry Hand Pies

....

Makes 8 hand pies

....

filling

1 pound (453g) fresh boysenberries

1 cup (200g) granulated sugar

¼ cup (35g) cornstarch

Zest and juice of 1 blood orange

Generous pinch kosher salt

to assemble

1 recipe Flaky Butter Crust (page 234)

All-purpose flour, for rolling

1 large egg, beaten, or 3 tablespoons
    buttermilk, for brushing

Coarse sanding sugar, for sprinkling

note: Make the Flaky Butter Crust
2 to 24 hours in advance, as it needs
to chill before you roll it out.

This filling is easily adapted for
other fruits: Blueberries, rhubarb,
and raspberries are all excellent with
blood orange juice. You can substitute
navel orange, lemon, or lime juice
if blood oranges are not available.

Boysenberries have a short season and a short shelf life, but they pack a ton of flavor and aroma into that time every year. They make the most intense berry-flavored hand pies, perfect for taking to a picnic or keeping in a sealed container on the counter for a quick treat. Although the seasons do not overlap, one of my favorite farmers always has blood oranges during the same time that the boysenberries become available. I love the gentle acid and berry-like flavors of blood oranges and they pair well with the boysenberries. They are especially appropriate here since the color of the juice closely matches the berries.

....

1. **Make the filling:** Combine the boysenberries, sugar, cornstarch, orange zest and juice, and salt in a large saucepan over medium heat and cook until the juices start to release from the fruit, about 5 minutes. Stir the fruit often to prevent it from sticking to the bottom of the pan. Bring the fruit to a simmer and allow the juices to thicken to a loose jam consistency, 3 minutes. Remove the filling from the heat and allow it to cool to room temperature before using.

2. **Assemble the hand pies:** Line two baking sheets with parchment paper.

3. If your dough has been chilled overnight, it will need to sit at room temperature a bit before rolling—this will take 10 to 15 minutes. Divide each disc into 4 pieces. Lightly flour your work surface and roll out each piece into a 7-inch roundish shape, just shy of ¼ inch thick. Transfer the rounds to the prepared baking sheets, 4 to a pan. Paint the edges of the dough with some of the beaten egg.

4. Mound a scant ¼ cup of the boysenberry filling in the center of each piece of dough. Fold the dough over the filling to meet the opposite edge in a half-moon shape and press the dough closed. Use a fork or your fingers to crimp the edges of the hand pies. Refrigerate or freeze until very cold, about 30 minutes.

5. Position two racks in the center zone of your oven and preheat the oven to 400°F.

6. Brush the tops of the hand pies with the remaining beaten egg and sprinkle with sanding sugar. Bake for about 30 minutes, until the crusts begin to brown. Reduce the oven temperature to 375°F. Bake for 15 more minutes, or until the crust is a deep golden brown. Transfer to a wire rack and let cool completely before serving. Store at room temperature in a sealed container for 1 day or up to 1 week in the fridge.

Sweet 100 Turnovers

Makes 8 turnovers

filling

½ pound (227g) Sweet 100 cherry tomatoes, or other very sweet, red cherry tomatoes

3 tablespoons sugar

3 tablespoons cornstarch

1 teaspoon freshly grated lemon zest

2 tablespoons fresh lemon juice

Generous pinch kosher salt

to assemble

All-purpose flour, for rolling

One 14-ounce (397g) package all-butter frozen puff pastry, thawed

1 large egg, beaten

Coarse sanding sugar, for sprinkling (optional)

The key to making tomatoes into something closer to dessert than dinner is using the ripest, sweetest varieties you can find. Sweet 100 tomatoes are notoriously candy-like and can be found easily at both farmer's markets and in grocery store aisles. Once you get them home, I find that most tomatoes need to continue ripening for at least a day outside of the fridge. Taste them for sweetness before using them in these unique, flaky pastries.

1. Make the filling: Combine the tomatoes, sugar, cornstarch, lemon zest, lemon juice, and salt in a large saucepan. Cook over medium heat, stirring often to prevent the mixture from sticking to the bottom of the pan, until the juices start to release from the tomatoes, about 5 minutes. Bring to a simmer and continue stirring until the juices thicken to a loose jam consistency, about 2 minutes. Remove the filling from the heat and allow it to cool to room temperature before using.

2. Assemble the turnovers: Position two racks in the center zone of your oven and preheat the oven to 400°F. Line two baking sheets with parchment paper.

3. Lightly flour your work surface and roll the pastry out to a 16 x 8-inch square. Cut the puff pastry into 8 squares. Divide the squares between the prepared baking sheets, arranging them several inches apart. Place 2 generous tablespoons of filling in the center of each piece of puff pastry. Brush the edges of each square with some of the beaten egg. Fold each square in half, enclosing the filling in a triangle-shaped pouch. Press and pinch the pastry edges with your fingertips to seal them tightly.

4. Brush the tops of the turnovers with the remaining beaten egg and sprinkle with sanding sugar, if desired. Bake for about 30 minutes, until the crusts begin to brown. Rotate the sheets top to bottom and front to back. Reduce the oven temperature to 375°F. Bake for 15 more minutes, or until the crust is a deep golden brown. Transfer the turnovers to a wire rack and let cool completely before serving. Store leftovers at room temperature for 1 day.

note: Thaw out your puff pastry according to the manufacturer's instructions before starting your turnovers.

Rhubarb Pie

....

Makes one 9½-inch pie

....

1 recipe Flaky Butter Crust (page 234)

3 tablespoons all-purpose flour, plus more for rolling

3 pounds (1359g) rhubarb, cut into 1-inch pieces

1½ cups (300g) granulated sugar

3 tablespoons fresh orange juice

1 teaspoon freshly grated orange zest

½ teaspoon vanilla bean paste or extract

2 tablespoons unsalted butter, room temperature

3 tablespoons heavy cream

1 tablespoon raw turbinado sugar

I have yet to find rhubarb from my local market that sends me over the moon with delight like the stuff they grow in Yorkshire, England. Grown in complete darkness, there the "pie" vegetable is forced from winter slumber by increasing the temperature inside the dark growing shed to a balmy 35°F, and then harvested by candlelight to ensure that no UV rays hit the signature acid-yellow leaves. The stalks range in color from palest pink to ruby red. Their bright hue is a direct result of the cold temperatures and the light starvation.

Forcing the plant also creates stalks that are shiny and smooth—unlike the hardier version grown outdoors—and the flavor is floral, almost tea-like. The process causes the stalks to grow so quickly that you can actually hear the sound of the plant expanding upwards. In the United States, forced-grown rhubarb can be difficult to find, mainly because rhubarb is not as popular here. Garden rhubarb is popular, and definitely worth the price if the stalks are in good condition. If you happen to get your hands on some shiny red stalks, I suggest making a pure rhubarb pie. After all the plant has been through, it deserves to stand on its own. If what's available near you is green and pale pink, you can always add a handful of strawberries to make up for the lack of color!

....

1. Remove the pie dough from the fridge and remove the plastic from each disc. If your dough has been chilled overnight, it will need to sit at room temperature a bit before rolling—this will take 10 to 15 minutes. Line a baking sheet with parchment paper.

2. Lightly flour a flat work surface and roll 1 disc of the pie dough out to a 12-inch round that is ⅛ inch thick. Transfer the dough to a 9½-inch pie dish and use your fingertips to relax the dough into the shape of the pie dish, leaving a 2-inch overhang around the edge of the dish. Roll the second disc of dough out to a 10-inch round and transfer it to the prepared baking sheet. Refrigerate the bottom and top crust until very cold, 15 to 25 minutes.

3. Combine the flour, rhubarb, granulated sugar, orange juice, orange zest, and vanilla in a large mixing bowl. Toss together and let the mixture stand for 5 minutes. Remove the top and bottom crusts from the refrigerator.

recipe continues

note: Make the Flaky Butter Crust 2 to 24 hours in advance, as it needs to chill before you roll it out.

4. Transfer the rhubarb filling with juices to the chilled pie shell. Dot the filling with the butter. Gently drape the top crust over the filling. Press the edges of the pie shell together to seal. Fold the edge of the pie dough under itself and crimp the edge of the crust with your thumb and forefinger, pressing gently into the pie dish as you crimp. Brush the top crust with the heavy cream and sprinkle with the turbinado sugar. Place the whole pie in the freezer for 15 minutes.

5. Position a rack in the center of your oven and preheat the oven to 400°F. Place a parchment-lined baking sheet on the lower rack to catch any juices that fall from the pie when it bakes.

6. Remove the pie from the freezer and cut a few slits in the top crust—this allows steam to escape from the filling while the pie bakes. Bake the pie for 30 minutes, reduce the temperature to 375°F, rotate the pie, and continue baking until the filling is bubbling and the crust is deeply golden brown, about 30 minutes more. Cool the pie on a wire rack for 2 hours before cutting. Store any leftovers at room temperature for 1 day or in the fridge for up to 1 week.

note: Make the Flaky Butter Crust 2 to 24 hours in advance, as it needs to chill before you roll it out.

Frankie's Lemon Pie

Makes one 9½-inch pie

½ recipe Flaky Butter Crust
(page 234)

3 tablespoons all-purpose flour,
plus more for rolling

1¾ cups (350g) sugar

3 tablespoons fine-ground yellow
cornmeal

½ teaspoon kosher salt

1 stick (113g) unsalted butter, melted
and cooled

5 large whole eggs plus 1 large egg yolk

1 tablespoon freshly grated lemon zest

1 cup (236ml) fresh lemon juice, from
about 4 to 6 medium-size lemons

My close friend Molly has a delicious little girl named Frankie (Frances). One hot August afternoon when Frankie was still a baby, her mother brought her to visit me at an outdoor market where I was selling pies. Frankie ate her first slice of pie (lemon chess) and said her first word ("MORE!"). So, now the Lemon Chess Pie is called Frankie's Lemon Pie.

1. Remove the pie dough from the fridge and remove the plastic wrap. If your dough has been chilled overnight, it will need to sit at room temperature a bit before rolling—this will take 10 to 15 minutes.

2. Lightly flour your work surface and roll the pie dough out to a 13-inch round that is ⅛ inch thick. Transfer to a 9½-inch pie dish and use your fingertips to relax the dough into the shape of the pie dish, leaving a 2-inch overhang around the edge of the dish. Fold the extra dough under itself. Use your thumb and forefinger to crimp the edge of the dough, pressing the dough into the pie dish and making sure the dough extends to the outer edge of the dish. This anchors the crust inside the dish, which results in a proud crown of crust after baking. Freeze the crimped crust for 20 minutes, until the dough is very cold.

3. Position a rack in the center of your oven and preheat the oven to 375°F.

4. Line the crust with heavy-duty foil, leaving a 1½-inch overhang. Trace your fingertips over the foil overhang and gently press it into the crimp. Fill the foil-lined crust with pie weights or dried beans. Bake for 20 to 25 minutes, until the crust is golden around the edges. Remove from the oven and lift out the foil and pie weights. Cool the crust completely.

5. Reduce the oven temperature to 325°F.

6. Combine the flour, sugar, cornmeal, and salt in a large mixing bowl. Make a well in the center of the flour mixture and add the melted butter, whole eggs, and yolk. Beat the mixture with a whisk until well combined; you can use an electric mixer for this step if you want. Add the lemon zest and juice and beat until the lemon juice has been fully incorporated.

7. Transfer the lemon filling to the cooled crust. Bake the pie until the filling is puffed at the edges and the center wobbles slightly when touched, 50 to 60 minutes. Cool the pie on a wire rack for at least 2 hours before slicing. Store leftovers at room temperature for 1 day or in the fridge for up to 1 week.

In Praise of Pears

"As it is, in my view, the duty of an apple to be crisp and crunchable,
a pear should have such a texture as leads to silent consumption . . ."

—Edward Ashdown Bunyard, *The Anatomy of Dessert*

Here is a story to tell your friends while you slice into a perfect, tender pear—if you have chosen the right variety, they will be able to hear you clearly above their silent chewing. The stage will be set for you to entertain them with the story of the Pear Mania of Massachusetts (1825–1875). Though Pear Mania took place in New England, it began percolating in the palaces of eighteenth-century Europe, where delicious, juicy pears were first discovered and made popular. Previous to the Renaissance, pears were mostly inedible, except when cooked, and mainly used to make cider (similar to the apple).

Pear growers had finally managed to breed the luxurious, dripping, honeyed pears that would soon drive royalty wild. In his book *The Fruit Hunters: A Story of Nature, Adventure, Commerce, and Obsession,* Adam Leith Gollner writes that a certain new variety of pear "Ah! Mon Dieu" was so delicious that upon eating the fruit, Louis XIV ejaculated. Must have been a *delicious* pear.

As these new varieties made their way to the New World, and the gentlemen of high society got hold of them, tasting parties began. Much in the same way that we now line up for limited edition beers, or even faddish pastries like the Cronut, these pears became the talk of the town. The new pear varieties caused an outbreak of flashy spending—men throwing money at

seeds and cuttings to start orchards. From this craze came at least one pear that we still see on the farmer's table. The Anjou was one of the hundreds of varieties of pears on display at the 1873 autumn fruit show of the Massachusetts Horticultural Society.

Here's the sad ending to the story: Pears are like apples in that the seeds do not guarantee an exact genetic match to the fruit they came from. So while many very rich men planted orchards of pear varieties from seed, many of those trees proved to be fruitless or undesirable and had to be destroyed. The great Pear Mania tapered off slowly, and we were left behind with only a few reliable varieties of pear that we can still enjoy today.

I can't imagine my baking life without the full perfume and texture of a ripe pear. I have always been a pear lover, with the exception of the crunchy Asian pear varieties that stumped me until very recently, when I simmered them in smoky mezcal and found their firm texture to be useful and delicious. But the pear continues to get a bad rap; it continues to be one of the least understood table fruits in America.

I assume that most people never enjoy a ripe pear because, like persimmons, they require more work than just picking them at the right time. Pears do not ripen on the tree. Instead they are grown to maturity and ripened after the fact. Eaters often assume the texture should be closer to an apple, and so they consume the fruit far too early and find it to be mostly disappointing. I agree with Edward Ashdown Bunyard: A ripe pear should yield to the bite with a silent, juicy resignation.

And pears are fragile figures. Even the more russet varieties have thin skins that are easily bruised. While they are related to apples, both being pome fruit in the rose family, they're very different in structure from apples. Pears are closer to quinces in that they contain granules in the flesh called sclereids, and they ripen from the inside out. This is the reason that you often see a dark circle around the core of a pear, and why you should test a pear's readiness by gently pressing the area around the stem. A ripe or almost-ripe pear will have a tenderness at the stem area and, if you've chosen an aromatic variety like the Bartlett, an unmistakably heady perfume.

Pear and Cranberry Pie

Makes one 9½-inch pie

1 recipe Flaky Butter Crust (page 234)

3 tablespoons all-purpose flour, plus more for rolling

6 large (3 pounds; 1359g) ripe-but-firm pears, peeled, cored, and cut into 2-inch chunks

¾ cup (150g) granulated sugar

½ cup (90g) fresh cranberries

¼ teaspoon ground cardamom

2 tablespoons unsalted butter

3 tablespoons heavy cream

1 tablespoon raw turbinado sugar

note: Make the Flaky Butter Crust 2 to 24 hours in advance, as it needs to chill before you roll it out.

Good-quality pears can have the most intoxicating aromas, and they begin to release their scents heavily when they get close to peak ripeness. They can be very sweet once cooked, often described as floral and honeyed, and I enjoy them the most when paired with something piquant, like cranberries or sharp cheese.

1. Remove the pie dough from the fridge and remove the plastic from each disc. If your dough has been chilled overnight, it will need to sit at room temperature a bit before rolling—this will take 10 to 15 minutes. Line a baking sheet with parchment paper.

2. Lightly flour a flat work surface and roll 1 disc of the pie dough out to a 12-inch round that is ⅛ inch thick. Transfer the dough to a 9½-inch pie dish and use your fingertips to relax the dough into the shape of the pie dish, leaving a 2-inch overhang around the edge of the dish. Roll the second disc of dough out to a 10-inch round and transfer it to the prepared baking sheet. Refrigerate the bottom and top crust until very cold, 15 to 25 minutes.

3. For the filling, combine the flour, pears, granulated sugar, cranberries, and cardamom in a large mixing bowl. Toss together and let the mixture stand for 5 minutes. Remove the top and bottom crusts from the refrigerator.

4. Transfer the filling to the chilled pie shell. Dot with the butter. Gently drape the top crust over the filling. Press the edges of the pie shell together to seal. Fold the edge of the pie dough under itself and crimp the edge of the crust with your thumb and forefinger, pressing gently into the pie dish as you crimp. Brush the top crust with the heavy cream and sprinkle with the turbinado sugar. Place the whole pie in the freezer for 15 minutes.

5. Position a rack in the center of your oven and preheat the oven to 400°F. Place a parchment-lined baking sheet on the lower rack to catch any juices that fall from the pie when it bakes.

6. Remove the pie from the freezer and cut a few slits in the top crust—this allows steam to escape from the filling while the pie bakes. Bake the pie for 30 minutes, reduce the heat to 375°F, rotate the pie, and continue baking until the filling is bubbling and the crust is deeply golden brown, about 30 minutes more.

7. Cool the pie on a wire rack for 2 hours before cutting. Store any leftovers at room temperature for 1 day or in the fridge for up to 1 week.

Honey-Glazed Strawberry Pie

....

Makes one 9½-inch pie

....

crust

All-purpose flour, for rolling

½ recipe Flaky Butter Crust (page 234)

glaze

1 cup (236ml) wildflower honey

¼ cup (59ml) apple juice

Juice of 1 lemon

to assemble

½ cup (112g) mascarpone cheese,
at room temperature

3 tablespoons granulated sugar

1 pound (453g) fresh strawberries,
hulled and quartered

2 cups (472ml) cold heavy whipping
cream

2 tablespoons confectioners' sugar

note: Make the Flaky Butter Crust 2 to
24 hours in advance, as it needs to chill
before you roll it out.

This pie requires a chilling time of
6 hours after it has been assembled.

The first time I made this pie at home, with the door to the back-yard wide open hoping to catch a breeze, I ended up luring in several wayward bees drawn to the scent of the cooking honey glaze. I was so annoyed by them that I ended up putting the entire pot of glaze outside and starting it over again, with the door closed.

....

1. If your dough has been chilled overnight, it will need to sit at room temperature for 10 to 15 minutes before rolling. Lightly flour your work surface and roll the pie dough out to a 13-inch round that is ⅛ inch thick. Transfer to a 9½-inch pie dish and use your fingertips to relax the dough into the shape of the pie dish, leaving a 2-inch overhang around the edge of the dish. Fold the extra dough under itself. Crimp the edge of the dough with your fingers, pressing the dough into the pie dish and making sure it extends to the outer edge of the dish. Freeze the crimped crust for about 20 minutes, until the dough is very cold.

2. Bake the crust: Position a rack in the center of your oven and preheat the oven to 375°F.

3. Line the crust with heavy-duty foil, leaving a 1½-inch overhang. Press the foil into the crimp. Fill the foil-lined crust with pie weights or dried beans. Bake for 20 to 25 minutes, until the crust is golden around the edges. Remove from the oven and lift out the foil and pie weights.

4. Return the crust to the oven and continue to bake until the inside crust is golden brown, about 15 minutes. Let cool.

5. Make the glaze: Combine the honey, apple juice, and lemon juice in a medium saucepan over medium heat and bring to a simmer. Simmer for 1 minute, then remove from the heat and let cool.

6. Assemble the pie: Combine the mascarpone cheese and granulated sugar in a small bowl. Spread the sweetened mascarpone cheese over the cooled crust. Add the strawberries to the pot of cooled glaze and stir them gently to coat. Pile the berries on top of the mascarpone.

7. In the bowl of an electric mixer fitted with the whisk attachment, combine the heavy cream and confectioners' sugar. Beat the cream on medium speed until soft but defined peaks form, about 3 minutes. Remove the whisk attachment and fold the cream a couple of turns with a spatula.

8. Pile the cream on top of the pie and swirl and swoosh it to your liking. Refrigerate the pie for 6 hours before serving, and store, refrigerated, for up to 3 days.

The Lime Pie That Saved Us

Makes one 9½-inch pie

1½ cups (128g) graham cracker crumbs

2 tablespoons sugar

1 teaspoon kosher salt

4 tablespoons unsalted butter, melted and cooled

One 14-ounce (414ml) can sweetened condensed milk

4 large egg yolks

1 tablespoon freshly grated lime zest

½ cup (118ml) fresh lime juice, from about 4 to 6 medium-sized limes

1 cup (236ml) cold heavy whipping cream

¼ cup (69g) sour cream

I opened my restaurant Fiona the week of Thanksgiving 2018. We became a destination for pie immediately, which was wonderful for us, but after the holiday was behind us things began to slow down a lot. We put this lime pie on the menu out of desperation—we needed an easy pie that held well in the fridge and wasn't dependent on fresh whole fruit, which was too expensive for us at the time, and this recipe fit that criteria. The lime pie caught the eye of famed food critic Bill Addison, who loved the pie so much he centered a review in the *LA Times* around it. This review came out one week after one of our most difficult weeks at Fiona. January is always a hard month in the restaurant world, and we were suffering financially. I had to make the hard decision to lay off several kitchen employees, and had gone weeks without being able to pay myself. I was at one of my lowest points (just writing this has me tearing up; the pressure and sadness of that few weeks is still with me) when Bill called the restaurant to tell us he was reviewing us, and to talk about pie. He loved the pie. The review posted, business quickly turned around, and pie sales—and sales across the board—increased. The lime pie saved us.

1. Preheat the oven to 325°F. Combine the graham cracker crumbs, sugar, salt, and melted butter in a mixing bowl and mix until moist crumbs form. Transfer the crumbly mixture to a 9½-inch pie plate and press into the bottom and up the sides of the pan. Bake for 10 minutes, or until lightly browned. Allow the crust to cool completely. Leave the oven on.

2. Combine the condensed milk, egg yolks, lime zest, and lime juice in a large mixing bowl. Whisk until the egg yolks have been incorporated and the zest is speckled throughout the mixture.

3. Transfer the lime filling to the cooled crust. Bake the pie until the filling is set at the edges and the center wobbles slightly when touched, about 15 minutes. Cool on a wire rack for at least 2 hours before slicing.

4. In the bowl of an electric mixer fitted with the whisk attachment, combine the heavy cream and sour cream. Beat the cream on medium speed until soft but defined peaks form, about 3 minutes.

5. Pile the cream on top of the pie and swirl and swoosh it to your liking. Refrigerate the pie for at least 3 hours before serving, and store, refrigerated, for up to 3 days.

Boiled Maple "Pumpkin" Pie

....

Makes one 9½-inch pie

....

1 pound (453g) kabocha squash, halved and seeded

½ recipe Flaky Butter Crust (page 234)

All-purpose flour, for rolling

1 cup (236ml) grade A dark color maple syrup

2 cups (472ml) heavy cream

1 teaspoon kosher salt

4 large eggs

2 teaspoons ground cinnamon

¼ teaspoon ground nutmeg

Freshly whipped cream for serving, optional

There are so many types of "pumpkins" available to us these days. In fall I see hubbard, red kuri, and kabocha squash at every farmer's market. Kabocha is one of the more readily available of the three. It's Japanese in origin and is reaching massive popularity, slowly pushing the butternut out of the spotlight. It has a rich, starchy flesh that when ripe is NEON orange. It's so vibrant in color, it dyes the plastic tubs we fill to the brim with maple pumpkin filling during the holiday season.

I incorporate these rich squashes into my daily diet when they are in season, so the idea of roasting one to make a superior pumpkin pie doesn't seem like such a daunting task. You could use canned pumpkin, but the flavor, color, and texture will not be the same.

....

1. Position a rack in the center of your oven and preheat the oven to 375°F. Wrap each kabocha squash half tightly in aluminum foil and bake until you can easily stick a fork into the squash, about 40 minutes. Unwrap the kabocha squash and let it cool completely. Scrape the orange flesh from the squash and discard the peel. Leave the oven on.

2. Remove the pie dough from the fridge and remove the plastic wrap. If your dough has been chilled overnight, it will need to sit at room temperature a bit before rolling—this will take 10 to 15 minutes. Lightly flour your work surface and roll the pie dough out to a 13-inch round that is ⅛ inch thick. Transfer to a 9½-inch pie dish and use your fingertips to relax the dough into the shape of the pie dish, leaving a 2-inch overhang around the edge of the dish. Fold the extra dough under itself. Use your thumb and forefinger to crimp the edge of the dough, pressing the dough into the pie dish and making sure the dough extends to the outer edge of the dish. This anchors the crust inside the dish, which results in a proud crown of crust after baking. Freeze the crimped crust for about 20 minutes, until the dough is very cold.

3. Line the crust with heavy-duty foil, leaving a 1½-inch overhang. Trace your fingertips over the foil overhang and gently press it into the crimp. Fill the foil-lined crust with pie weights or dried beans. Bake for 20 to 25 minutes, until the crust is golden around the edges. Remove from the oven and lift out the foil and pie weights. Cool the crust completely.

recipe continues

note: Make the Flaky Butter Crust 2 to 24 hours in advance, as it needs to chill before you roll it out.

4. Reduce the oven temperature to 325°F.

5. Put the maple syrup into a medium saucepan and bring it to a rolling boil over medium heat. Cook the maple syrup until a candy thermometer registers 235°F, about 10 minutes. Remove the pan from the heat and add the heavy cream and salt. Place the pan back on the stove over medium heat and bring it to a simmer. Remove from the heat and let cool for 15 minutes.

6. Combine the kabocha squash, eggs, cinnamon, and nutmeg in the carafe of a blender. Blend on high until very smooth. Reduce the speed to low and slowly stream in the maple caramel. Blend until combined.

7. Pour the filling into the prepared crust and bake the pie until the center of the custard wobbles a bit when the pie is gently jiggled, about 40 minutes. Cool the pie on a wire rack for 1 hour before serving. Serve the pie dolloped with whipped cream if you desire. Store leftovers in the fridge for up to 1 week.

Caramelized Pineapple Tarts

Makes 6 individual tarts

pineapple

¼ cup plus 1 tablespoon (62g) sugar

1 teaspoon vanilla bean paste or extract

Generous pinch kosher salt

1 large, ripe pineapple, peeled, cored, and cut into ½-inch cubes (about 1½ cups)

to assemble

1 recipe Pasta Frolla (page 238)

All-purpose flour, for rolling

¼ cup (59ml) heavy cream

1 large egg

¼ cup (56g) coarse sanding sugar

3 tablespoons unsweetened shredded coconut, for serving

½ cup (112g) crème fraiche, for serving

note: If pineapple isn't your thing, but you still appreciate dark caramel and salty-sweet flavors, you can easily substitute sour apples, apricots, or plums.

People (pineapple lovers) say that you've never really had pineapple until you've had one in Hawaii. I've had the pleasure of eating a pineapple on a sandy beach in Hawaii and I can verify that it is a true statement. They are sweeter and juicier and vibrant yellow (or gold—Maui Gold to be exact). Now, listen, I know that's not a thing we can all just run off and do this weekend. That's okay! That's bucket-list stuff! BUT *you can* learn how to choose a ripe pineapple at the market (look for yellow skin, smell the stem area for tropical aroma) and create your very own beach-party vibes with this caramelized pineapple dessert. Pineapples are like figs in that they don't ripen very much after being picked, so don't buy a green pineapple.

1. **Caramelize the pineapple:** Combine the sugar, vanilla, and salt in a large saucepan over medium heat. Place the pineapple cubes on top of the sugar. Cook undisturbed until the sugar has melted and begun to brown and the pineapple has released some juice, about 7 minutes. Remove from the heat and let cool in the pan to room temperature.

2. **Assemble the tarts:** Position a rack in the center of your oven and preheat the oven to 375°F. Line a baking sheet with parchment paper.

3. Divide the pasta frolla into 6 equal pieces. Roll each piece of dough out to a 7-inch round in between two sheets of lightly floured parchment paper. Place the dough rounds on the prepared baking sheet.

4. Mound a scant ¼ cup of the pineapple in the center of each portion of dough, reserving the juices in the pan for after baking. Fold the edges of the dough up around the filling in loose pleats, leaving the fruit exposed in the center of the tart.

5. Whisk the cream and egg together and brush each of the tarts generously with the mixture. Sprinkle the tarts with the coarse sugar. Snuggle any extra pineapple cubes inside the open space on the tart.

6. Bake until the tarts are golden brown and the pineapple juices bubble up in the opening of each pie, about 45 minutes. While they're still hot, paint the tops with the reserved liquid. Cool the tarts on a wire rack until ready to serve. Sprinkle the shredded coconut over the tarts and serve warm with a dollop of cold crème fraiche. Store at room temperature in a sealed container for 1 day or up to 1 week in the fridge

Rhubarb Tarte Tatin

......

Makes one 10-inch tarte

......

½ recipe Flaky Butter Crust (page 234)

All-purpose flour, for rolling

1 cup (200g) packed dark brown sugar

1 stick (113g) good-quality, grass-fed unsalted butter

1 teaspoon vanilla bean paste or extract

Pinch kosher salt

2 pounds (906g) rhubarb, cut into 2-inch pieces

Freshly whipped cream, for serving (optional)

I was surprised to bite into this delectable, caramelized tarte Tatin and find that rhubarb is the perfect vehicle for the transport of true butter flavor. The bright acidity of the rhubarb acts much like lemon in a buttery sauce. It makes the butter taste more like butter. When you serve the traditional apple version, you would usually accompany it with a dollop of whipped cream. Same goes for this version, although it doesn't really need it!

....

1. Position a rack in the center of your oven and preheat the oven to 400°F. Line a baking sheet with parchment paper.

2. Remove the pie dough from the fridge and remove the plastic wrap. If your dough has been chilled overnight, it will need to sit at room temperature a bit before rolling—this will take 10 to 15 minutes. Lightly flour your work surface and roll the pie dough out to a 13-inch round that is ⅛ inch thick. Transfer the dough to the prepared baking sheet and chill until ready to use.

3. Place a 10-inch cast-iron skillet over medium heat. When the skillet is hot, combine the brown sugar, butter, vanilla, and salt in the skillet. As the sugar and butter melt, swirl the mixture around to coat the bottom of the pan. Cook until the sugar has completely melted and the mixture boils vigorously, about 10 minutes. Remove the skillet from the heat and let it cool for 5 minutes.

4. Remove the crust from the refrigerator. Arrange the rhubarb pieces in the skillet, covering the entire bottom of the pan and squeezing in as many as you can. Lay the crust over the rhubarb and fold the extra dough at the sides of the pan over onto itself to create a ring around the tarte.

5. Bake until the crust is a deep golden brown and the juices bubble at the edges of the skillet, about 45 minutes. Remove the skillet from the oven and allow the tarte to cool for 20 minutes. Loosen the crust with a paring knife. Place a serving plate on top of the skillet and, holding onto it with oven gloves or a thick kitchen towel, carefully invert the skillet to release the tarte. Serve warm, with the whipped cream, if desired. Store leftovers at room temperature for 1 day.

note: Make the Flaky Butter Crust 2 to 24 hours in advance, as it needs to chill before you roll it out.

Prune and Pistachio Cream Tart

....

Makes one 13¾ x 4½ x 1-inch tart

....

Unsalted butter, for greasing

½ recipe Pistachio Pasta Frolla
(page 239)

1 teaspoon all-purpose flour, plus more
for rolling

2 pounds (906g) fresh prunes, halved
and pitted

3 tablespoons honey

Generous pinch kosher salt

1 recipe Pistachio Cream (page 247)

Lifelong prune appreciator here. I raise my hand to proudly proclaim my love for prunes, especially fresh prunes. I love the dusty, moody color of the skin that hides the translucent neon yellow-green interior. I love them raw and cooked and dried. In this tart, I pair them with pistachio for both visual and palate excitement.

....

1. Lightly butter a 13¾ x 4½ x 1-inch fluted tart pan with a removable bottom.

2. Remove the dough from the fridge. Remove the plastic and lightly dust the dough with flour. Place the dough on a piece of parchment paper and knead it a few times to loosen it up. Transfer the dough to the prepared pan and press the dough into the pan. Press evenly across the bottom and up the sides of the pan. Once you have a uniform shell of roughly ¼-inch thickness, prick the bottom of the dough several times with a fork. Freeze the tart shell for at least 30 minutes, until the dough is very cold and firm.

3. Position a rack in the center of your oven and preheat the oven to 350°F. Line the chilled shell with parchment paper and fill with pie weights or dried beans. Put the tart pan on a baking sheet and bake for 20 to 25 minutes, until the shell is golden around the edges. Remove from the oven and lift out the parchment paper and pie weights. Let the baked shell cool for 20 minutes before continuing. Line a baking sheet with parchment paper.

4. Once the tart shell has cooled to warm room temperature, toss the prunes with the flour, honey, and salt in a medium bowl. Spread the pistachio cream over the bottom of the shell, then arrange the prunes on top of the cream, packing in every last piece of fruit. Place the tart on the prepared baking sheet. Bake until the fruit is bubbling and caramelized and the crust is golden brown, about 45 minutes. Some juices might escape and jump overboard—that's what the lined baking sheet is for.

5. Allow the tart to cool to a warm room temperature before cutting. It will keep well at room temperature for 1 day or in the fridge for 1 week.

note: Make sure to chill the Pistachio Pasta Frolla for 30 minutes before using.
    You can substitute many different fruits here: apricots or tart green apples would be perfect with the pistachio cream.

Strawberry Galettes

....

*Makes 8
individual-size galettes*

....

1 recipe Flaky Butter Crust (page 234), undivided

All-purpose flour, for rolling

1 pound (453g) fresh strawberries, hulled and quartered

2 cups (400g) Vanilla Bean Sugar (page 228)

2 tablespoons cornstarch

Zest of 1 lemon

½ teaspoon kosher salt

½ cup (118ml) heavy cream

1 large egg, beaten, or 3 tablespoons buttermilk, for brushing

Coarse sanding sugar, for sprinkling

note: Make the Flaky Butter Crust 2 to 24 hours in advance so that it can be properly chilled prior to rolling.

A basic knowledge of galette construction means that you can adapt these to pretty much any fruit. Juicier fruits such as other berries, cherries, or very ripe stone fruits need the thickening agent more so than a classic apple galette (you can reduce the cornstarch to 2 teaspoons for apples). Try a version with a base layer of Almond Cream (page 247) spread over the bottom of the dough before arranging the fruit—it adds richness and height to the rustic dessert.

Cooked strawberries are a controversial subject in some circles. I love them, but I agree that there is a right way to cook them. My method is simple enough: Cook them hard and dark. They are at their best when you choose a high-flavor variety with good color, and you cook them until nearly all the water has escaped and they are concentrated and toothsome. Anything less than that and you have the soft, pallid, slippery fruit situation that gives cooked strawberries a bad name.

....

1. Line two baking sheets with parchment paper.

2. Divide the pie dough into 8 equal-size pieces. If your dough has been chilled overnight, it will need to sit at room temperature a bit before rolling—this will take 10 to 15 minutes. Lightly flour your work surface and roll out each piece to a 7-inch round (or something close to round) just shy of ¼-inch thickness. Transfer the dough rounds to the prepared baking sheets, placing 4 on each sheet.

3. In a large bowl, combine the strawberries, vanilla sugar, cornstarch, lemon zest, and salt. Place a heaping ⅓ cup of the berry mixture on each dough round, leaving a 1½-inch border. Fold the edges of the dough up over the filling in loose pleats, leaving the fruit exposed in the center of each galette. Gently arrange the galettes on the baking sheets so they're several inches from one another.

4. Refrigerate or freeze the galettes until the dough is firm, about 20 minutes in the fridge or 10 minutes in the freezer.

5. Position two racks in the center zone of your oven and preheat the oven to 400°F.

6. Pour 1 tablespoon of cream in the opening of each galette. Brush the edges of the dough with the egg and sprinkle each galette with sanding sugar.

7. Reduce the heat to 375°F. Bake until the crusts are golden brown, about 30 minutes. Rotate the pans top to bottom and front to back and continue to bake until the juices bubble from the center of each galette, about 15 minutes more. Transfer to a wire rack and let the galettes cool completely before serving. Store at room temperature in a sealed container for 1 day or up to 1 week in the fridge.

Apricot Galette

Makes one 10-inch galette

1 recipe Flaky Whole-Wheat Crust
(page 237), undivided

All-purpose flour, for rolling

2 pounds (906g) fresh apricots

½ cup (100g) granulated sugar

3 tablespoons cornstarch

½ teaspoon kosher salt

3 tablespoons heavy cream

Coarse sanding sugar, for sprinkling

2 tablespoons apricot preserves,
for decoration (optional)

½ teaspoon dried lavender flowers
(optional)

The season for perfect, intensely flavored, not-mealy apricots seems to last two days in Los Angeles, and most years I miss the magic window and settle for imperfect seconds. Every year, I look to re-create the apricots of my youth, when I ate them from a tree in our neglected backyard. The hot, dry weather concentrated the flavor, and they were always left to ripen on the tree because no one cared to pick them. I rarely find that apricot, but I remain hopeful.

A note about using the kernel of an apricot as a flavoring agent: Apricot kernels contain amygdalin, which the body converts to cyanide. Amygdalin is present in the seeds of many fruits—apples, for example. Using the kernels of the fruit to impart an almond flavor in pastries and ice creams has been common practice for a long time, but if the idea of using them makes you nervous, omit them or substitute them with almond extract. Some bakers believe that cooking the pits breaks down the amygdalin and makes it inactive, which is why they feel you can safely use it to flavor your baked goods.

1. Line a baking sheet with parchment paper.

2. Remove the pie dough from the fridge and remove the plastic wrap. If your dough has been chilled overnight, it will need to sit at room temperature a bit before rolling—this will take 10 to 15 minutes. Lightly flour your work surface and roll the pie dough out to a 13-inch round that is ⅛ inch thick. Transfer the dough to the prepared baking sheet.

3. Cut each apricot into quarters and remove the pits. Reserve 6 pits to season the filling. (Save the rest for making ice cream or custard. The pits can be dried and kept at room temperature for up to a year.) Set the apricots aside. Place the apricot pits in a mortar and pestle and lightly tap each pit to break the hard outer shell (you don't want to shatter the pit completely, as it makes extracting the kernel difficult). After each pit has been broken open, remove the soft almond-like kernel from the center. Discard the shells.

4. Return the apricot kernels to the mortar and pestle and smash them into a paste. Transfer the paste to a large mixing bowl and add the granulated sugar. Mix with your hands to combine.

recipe continues

5. Add the apricot quarters, cornstarch, and salt to the bowl and toss to coat.

6. Arrange the apricots on the prepared crust: Starting in the center, place the apricots cut-sides up in a spiral on the pastry round, leaving a 3-inch border at the edge. If you still have apricots once you have covered the center of the pastry, wedge the rest of the apricots in between and around the edge. Use all the fruit!

7. Fold the edges of the dough up over the filling in loose pleats, leaving an open hole no larger than 6 inches in the center of the galette. Refrigerate the galette until the pastry is firm, about 30 minutes.

8. Position a rack in the center of your oven and preheat the oven to 400°F.

9. Brush the edges of the pastry with the heavy cream and sprinkle with sanding sugar. Bake for 30 minutes, or until the crust begins to brown. Reduce the oven temperature to 375°F, rotate the baking sheet and continue baking until the juices bubble in the center of the galette and the apricots begin to caramelize, about 30 minutes more. Remove the galette from the oven and allow it to cool on the baking sheet for 30 minutes, then transfer it to a wire rack and cool completely.

10. If desired, mix the apricot preserves with 1 teaspoon of hot water. Brush the apricot filling with the preserves to get a luscious, shiny surface. Garnish with the dried lavender flowers, if using. Serve warm. Store leftovers at room temperature for 1 day.

Provençal-Style Cheesecake

·········

Serves 10 to 12

········

crust

3 tablespoons unsalted butter, melted, plus more for greasing

2 cups (192g) fine-ground almond flour

¼ cup (31g) all-purpose flour

3 tablespoons packed dark brown sugar

filling

One 8-ounce (227g) package cream cheese, at room temperature

6 ounces (170g) fresh goat cheese, at room temperature

1½ cups (345g) sour cream

4 large eggs

1½ cups (300g) granulated sugar

strawberry topping

1 pound (453g) fresh strawberries, hulled and quartered

3 tablespoons honey

¼ teaspoon vanilla bean paste or extract

Inspired by a wonderful trip to Provence, I've added goat cheese in place of fromage blanc. Fresh goat cheese is a specialty in the South of France and pairs well with fresh fruit.

···

1. Make the crust: Position a rack in the center of your oven and preheat the oven to 350°F. Lightly butter a 9-inch round springform pan.

2. Combine the melted butter, almond flour, all-purpose flour, and brown sugar in a mixing bowl and mix until moist crumbs form. Transfer the crumbly mixture to the prepared springform pan and press into the bottom and about 2 inches up the sides of the pan. Bake for 20 minutes, or until lightly browned. Allow the crust to cool completely. Leave the oven on.

3. Make the filling: Put the cream cheese in the bowl of an electric mixer fitted with the paddle attachment. Beat on medium speed until it is very smooth and fluffy, about 2 minutes. Add the goat cheese and sour cream and continue mixing until incorporated. With the mixer running, add the eggs 1 at a time, mixing thoroughly after each addition. Scrape down the bottom and sides of the bowl. Add the granulated sugar and continue to beat on medium speed until the mixture is very fluffy, about an additional 3 minutes.

4. Wrap the bottom of the springform pan in plastic wrap, then cut a large square of foil and wrap the outside of the pan with it, plastic wrap and all. This will keep unwanted water from creeping its way into the springform pan as it bakes in the water bath, and prevent a soggy-bottomed crust. In a medium saucepan, bring 4 cups (944ml) water to a boil. Remove the water from the heat, and set it aside.

5. Transfer the filling to the prepared crust. Place the springform pan in a roasting pan large enough to hold the springform and at least 2 inches of water. Place the roasting pan in the oven and carefully pour the hot water into the roasting pan. It should reach about halfway up the sides of the springform pan.

6. Bake the cheesecake until the edges brown lightly and the center wobbles a little when gently touched, about 45 minutes. Remove the cheesecake from the water bath and let it cool to room temperature on a wire rack. You can chill the cheesecake at this point if you would like to serve it cold, or serve it at room temperature, which is how I prefer it. Keep the oven on for the topping.

recipe continues

7. Make the topping: Place the berries in a 13 x 9-inch baking dish and toss them with the honey and vanilla. Bake until the strawberries are juicy and a little caramelized, about 25 minutes, stirring several times throughout. Remove the strawberries from the oven and let them cool to room temperature. If you're serving the cheesecake cold, store the strawberries separate from the cake.

8. When you are ready to serve, remove the springform pan and transfer the cheesecake to a cake plate or stand. Spoon the roasted strawberries over the cheesecake. Any leftovers will keep well in the fridge for up to 1 week.

Provençal Style

Smack-dab in the middle of writing this book, I took a summer trip to Provence with my friend whose family had rented a house in a small town called Saint-Pantaléon. We spent our days swimming, shopping at outdoor markets, and cooking lovely dinners for one another. On my first night, I lay in my bed unraveling the bountiful scenes of that day, the countless grape vines, cherry trees, and apple orchards we passed on the way to the market. The baskets of stone fruits and teensy-tiny strawberries in the market. As I drifted off to sleep, already in love with this special place, the cicadas clicked and clacked in an oak tree outside my window.

I made many delicious things while in Provence, and on my last night I helped make dinner with the neighbors and owners of the house, Alexandre and Louise. Alexandre begged for an "American-style cheesecake" and I could not turn him down. We didn't have cream cheese, but we had crème fraiche and fromage blanc from the local dairy, and almond flour for an on-the-fly crust.

They grow a lot of almonds in that region, so our almond-flour crust became an expression of the earth that produces all the wonderful fruit. The fromage blanc was fresh and tangy, and the crème fraiche was rich. We used the last of a basket of local strawberries for a topping. What we created was not even close to an American-style cheesecake, and for that I apologize to Alexandre. What we ended up making was a cheesecake that was very Provençal style.

Ice Creams and Sorbets

Brown Sugar Apricot Kernel Ice Cream

Black Raspberry Ice Cream

Whole Tangerine Sorbet

Blackberry Frozen Yogurt

Roasted Fig Frozen Yogurt

Cherimoya and Green Tea Ice Cream

Caramel Banana Ice Cream

Green Melon and Tomato Granita

Peach Melba Sundaes

Raspberry Campari Sorbet

Brown Sugar Apricot Kernel Ice Cream

Makes about 2 quarts

8 apricot pits

1½ cups (354ml) whole milk

¾ cup (177ml) heavy cream

1 cup (236ml) canned evaporated milk

4 large egg yolks

½ cup (100g) packed dark brown sugar

3 tablespoons cornstarch

¼ teaspoon kosher salt

1 tablespoon brandy

note: I infuse the apricot kernels in the cream and milk overnight for maximum flavor extraction. You can get a moderate amount of flavor after 6 hours, and if you haven't had apricot kernels before, you may prefer the shorter time. Taste the infused cream after a few hours and see where it is at; just know that colder temperatures dull flavors. If you have concern over the use of apricot kernels in baking and cooking, please read page 181 for some thoughts about it. You can omit them altogether and substitute ½ teaspoon almond extract after the custard has been cooked.

While this recipe does not contain actual fruit, it is a perfect accompaniment to ripe fruit in the form of a simple sundae. The natural almond essence of the apricot kernel is the poor man's almond extract, and cracking the pits open is quite therapeutic.

1. Place the apricot pits in a mortar and pestle and lightly tap each pit to break the shell (you don't want to shatter the pit completely, as it makes extracting the kernel difficult). After each pit has been broken open, remove the soft almond-like kernel from the center. Discard the shells. Return the apricot kernels to the mortar and pestle and smash them into a paste. In a medium saucepan over medium heat, combine the apricot kernels with the whole milk, cream, and evaporated milk. Bring the mixture to a boil then remove from the heat and cool to room temperature. Once the milk mixture has cooled, transfer to an airtight container and refrigerate to continue the infusion overnight.

2. The next day, remove the milk mixture from the refrigerator and pour it into a large saucepan. Bring the mixture to a boil, then remove from the heat and strain out the kernels.

3. Fill a large bowl with ice cubes and cold water and set a clean bowl inside it. Have a fine-mesh strainer handy.

4. In a separate bowl, combine the egg yolks, brown sugar, cornstarch, and salt. Pour ¼ cup of the hot milk mixture into the egg mixture to temper the eggs, and whisk. Add the rest of the milk mixture and mix to combine, then return to the large saucepan and cook, stirring constantly, over medium-low heat until a silky custard forms and coats the back of a spoon, about 5 minutes. Make sure to scrape the bottom of the pan frequently.

5. Strain the custard into the bowl inside the prepared ice bath. Stir the custard to cool it to 40°F, until it is very cold. Alternately you can cool the custard to room temperature and refrigerate it overnight or for at least 6 hours before churning it.

6. Add the brandy to the custard and transfer the mixture to the bowl of a 2-quart capacity ice cream maker. Freeze according to the manufacturer's instructions. Transfer the ice cream to an airtight container and chill it in the freezer for at least 4 to 5 hours before serving.

Black Raspberry Ice Cream

Makes about 2 quarts

custard

1½ cups (354ml) whole milk

½ cup (118ml) canned evaporated milk

4 large egg yolks

¾ cup (150g) sugar

3 tablespoons cornstarch

¼ teaspoon kosher salt

1½ cups (336g) crème fraiche or sour cream

fruit puree

2½ cups (313g) fresh black or red raspberries

1 cup (200g) sugar

I was taken by surprise when I ate my first scoop of black-raspberry ice cream at the local dairy in New Hampshire and realized it was a completely new fruit to me. It was not blackberry flavored but definitely not red raspberry, either. It was much softer than both and distinctly floral tasting. There really isn't a substitution for them, but this base makes a great red raspberry ice cream if you can't find black raspberries at your market.

. . . .

1. **Make the custard:** Fill a large bowl with ice cubes and cold water and set a clean medium-size bowl inside it. Have a fine-mesh strainer handy.

2. Heat the whole milk and evaporated milk in a large saucepan over medium heat until the mixture is hot to the touch and steam rises from the surface, about 7 minutes. Do not boil it.

3. In a separate bowl, combine the egg yolks, sugar, cornstarch, and salt. Pour ¼ cup of the hot milk mixture into the egg mixture and whisk. Add the rest of the milk mixture and mix to combine, then return to the large saucepan. Cook, stirring constantly, over medium-low heat until a silky custard forms and coats the back of a spoon, about 4 minutes. Make sure to scrape the bottom of the pan frequently.

4. Strain the custard into the bowl inside the prepared ice bath. Stir the custard to cool it to 40°F, until it is very cold. Alternately you can cool the custard to room temperature and refrigerate it overnight or for at least 6 hours before continuing. Place the custard in the refrigerator while you make the puree.

5. **Make the puree:** Prepare another ice bath. Empty the ice and water from the large bowl and refill it with fresh ice cubes and cold water. Set a clean bowl inside it.

6. Place 2 cups of the black raspberries in a blender and puree. Strain the puree through a fine-mesh strainer into a small saucepan. Add the sugar to the saucepan and bring the mixture to a boil over medium heat. Add the remaining whole berries and boil for 1 minute more. Remove from the heat and transfer the mixture to the bowl inside the ice bath. Cool the puree until it is very cold, about 40°F. Whisk in the crème fraiche.

7. Add the fruit puree to the custard and transfer to the bowl of a 2-quart-capacity ice cream maker. Freeze according to the manufacturer's instructions. Transfer the ice cream to an airtight container and chill it in the freezer for at least 4 to 5 hours before serving.

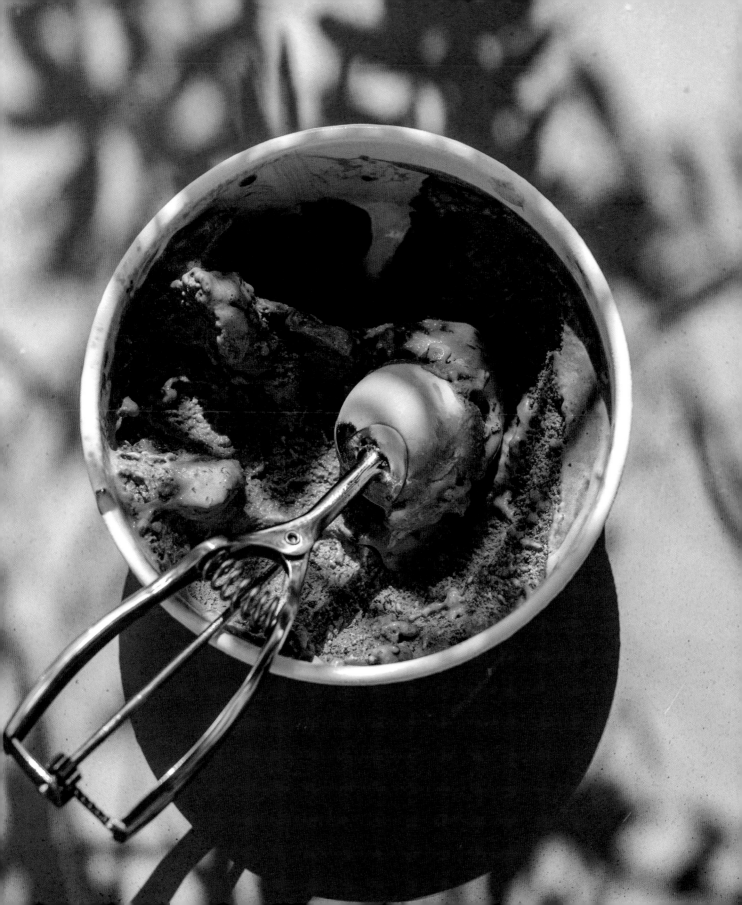

Whole Tangerine Sorbet

Makes about 2 quarts

3 pounds (1359g) small sweet
   tangerines (about 15)

1 cup (200g) sugar

Pinch kosher salt

We have a big tangerine tree of unknown variety in our backyard. The first year we lived in the house, the tree came to life in winter and gave us a few good bowls of fruit. It's an old tree. We figured we would leave it for shade and just let it be. My husband set to improving the yard, digging up hard-packed dirt and enriching the soil nearby, and after that first winter, we saw a difference. The tree was improving, and we started feeding and watering it regularly. It's paying off. Last winter, the old-man tree gave us more than one hundred pounds of fruit. We have plenty to juice and to share with friends, and to make this super-charged whole-tangerine sorbet. The skin from the tangerines contains pectin, which aids in keeping the sorbet smooth after you freeze it. It also adds an intense citrus flavor and aroma.

1. Peel all but 4 of the tangerines. Place the peeled tangerines and sugar in a blender or the bowl of a food processor and puree until the sugar has completely dissolved. Strain the juice through a fine-mesh strainer or cheesecloth into a large measuring cup. Discard the pulp. You should have 3 cups of tangerine juice.

2. Fill a medium bowl with ice cubes and cold water. Place the remaining 4 tangerines in a small saucepan and cover them with water. Bring to a boil over medium heat, then turn the heat down to medium-low and simmer the tangerines until they are fork tender, about 15 minutes. Place the cooked tangerines in the ice bath and cool them completely.

3. Cut each cooked tangerine in half and remove the seeds. Cut the halves, peels and all, into smaller chunks, about 1-inch pieces. Place the pieces (peels and all) in the bowl of a food processor fitted with the blade attachment and puree until smooth. Pour in the sweetened juice and blend until combined. Strain the mixture into the bowl of a 2-quart-capacity ice cream maker. Freeze according to the manufacturer's instructions. Transfer the sorbet to an airtight container and chill it in the freezer for at least 4 to 5 hours before serving.

Blackberry Frozen Yogurt

Makes about 2 quarts

2½ cups (275g) fresh blackberries

1 cup (236ml) wildflower honey (or a bit less if you like it tart—just keep in mind that less honey makes for an icier frozen yogurt)

3 tablespoons fresh lemon juice

1½ cups (338g) full-fat plain yogurt (use any tart, loose yogurt)

1½ cups (341g) full-fat plain Greek yogurt

¼ teaspoon kosher salt

½ teaspoon orange blossom water

It may seem fussy to blend two different yogurts to make this classic frozen treat, but I have my reasons. I love the tangy flavor of unstrained yogurt and the texture and creaminess of Greek-style yogurt. When I set out to make the perfect homespun fro-yo, I knew the finished product had to be both tangy and creamy. Any berry could be subbed for blackberries, but this is my favorite version of this recipe.

1. Fill a large bowl with ice cubes and cold water and set a clean bowl inside it. Have a fine-mesh strainer handy. Place the blackberries and honey in a small saucepan and smash them with a fork or potato masher. Add the lemon juice and bring the mixture to a simmer over medium heat. Allow the fruit to simmer for 5 minutes, just until softened. Remove from the heat and pass the mixture through the strainer and into the bowl inside the prepared ice bath. Cool the fruit mixture in the ice bath until the mixture registers at least 40°F on an instant-read thermometer. Alternately you can cool the mixture to room temperature and refrigerate it overnight or for at least 6 hours.

2. Whisk the yogurts, berry mixture, salt, and orange blossom water together in a large mixing bowl.

3. Transfer the mixture to the bowl of a 2-quart-capacity ice cream maker and freeze according to the manufacturer's instructions. Transfer the frozen yogurt to an airtight container and chill it in the freezer for at least 4 to 5 hours before serving.

Roasted Fig Frozen Yogurt

....

Makes about 2 quarts

....

1 pound (453g) fresh ripe figs, halved and stemmed

⅔ cup (158ml) wildflower honey

1½ cups (338g) full-fat plain yogurt (use any tart, loose yogurt)

1½ cups (341g) full-fat plain Greek yogurt

3 tablespoons fresh lemon juice

¼ teaspoon kosher salt

If you have a fig tree, you know what work they can be. They grow largely unattended, but if you want to eat anything from them, it becomes you against the birds when late summer rolls around. Birds love taking bites of unripe figs and leaving them on the tree to rot. Once the figs begin to rot, the Figeater Beetles arrive and eat the fermented fruit—they deter some people from picking the ripe figs because they are loud, blind, and love landing on your head, which can be unsettling! Because figs ripen only on the tree, getting perfect ripe fruit can be a real challenge. I have resorted to nets, checking them daily for sneaky birds that may have got caught in the nets' weave. When I do get enough figs for a batch of frozen yogurt, I really feel like I have earned it.

....

1. Position a rack in the center of your oven and preheat the oven to 350°F.

2. Place the figs cut-sides up in a single layer inside a 13 x 9-inch ceramic or glass baking dish. Drizzle the honey over the figs and roast until the flesh of the figs begins to caramelize and the juices have begun to thicken in the bottom of the dish, about 15 minutes. Remove from the oven and let cool to room temperature.

3. Fill a large bowl with ice cubes and cold water and set a clean medium-size bowl inside it. Place the cooled figs and any juices from the baking dish in the bowl of a food processor fitted with the blade attachment. Blend the figs for a few seconds, until they are broken up into a chunky mush. Add the yogurts, lemon juice, and salt to the food processor and process just until the yogurts are mixed into the figs. Pour the mixture into the bowl inside the prepared ice bath and stir until the mixture registers 40°F on an instant-read thermometer. Alternately you can cool the mixture to room temperature and refrigerate it overnight or for at least 6 hours.

4. Transfer the mixture to the bowl of a 2-quart-capacity ice cream maker and freeze according to the manufacturer's instructions. Transfer the frozen yogurt to an airtight container and chill it in the freezer for at least 4 to 5 hours before serving.

Cherimoya and Green Tea Ice Cream

Makes about 2 quarts

2 cups (472ml) heavy cream

1 cup (236ml) whole milk

1 tablespoon matcha powder

4 large egg yolks

½ cup (100g) sugar

3 tablespoons cornstarch

Pinch of kosher salt

1 cup (250g) 1-inch pieces ripe peeled and seeded cherimoya, frozen solid

Nicknamed the ice cream fruit, cherimoya can sometimes be found at farmer's markets in Southern California. It is still a relatively rare breed of fruit tree, and often don't produce fruit for up to ten or more years. Cherimoyas are an esoteric and exotic delicacy. On the tree, they look like big, green dinosaur hearts hanging in between heart-shaped leaves. You can eat cherimoyas out of hand with a spoon—they're creamy and sweet. I like making actual ice cream with cherimoya, it adds a tropical note, and in this recipe it balances the bitterness of matcha.

1. Fill a large bowl with ice cubes and cold water and set a clean medium-size bowl inside it. Have a fine-mesh strainer handy.

2. Heat the cream and milk in a large saucepan over medium heat until the mixture is hot to the touch and steam rises from the surface, about 4 minutes. Do not boil it. Whisk in the matcha and remove from the heat.

3. In a separate bowl, combine the egg yolks, sugar, cornstarch, and salt. Pour ¼ cup of the hot milk mixture into the egg mixture and whisk. Add the rest of the milk mixture and mix to combine, then return to the large saucepan and cook, stirring constantly, over medium-low heat until a silky custard forms and coats the back of a spoon, about 5 minutes. Make sure to scrape the bottom of the pan frequently.

4. Strain the custard into the bowl inside the prepared ice bath. Stir the custard to cool it to 40°F on an instant-read thermometer. Alternately you can cool the mixture to room temperature and refrigerate it overnight or for at least 6 hours.

5. Place the cherimoya in a blender or the bowl of a food processor and puree until very smooth. Add the fruit to the custard and transfer the mixture to the bowl of a 2-quart-capacity ice cream maker. Freeze according to the manufacturer's instructions. Transfer the ice cream to an airtight container and chill it in the freezer for at least 4 to 5 hours before serving.

note: If you are using fresh cherimoya, you will need to freeze the fruit until solid. Overnight is best.

Caramel Banana Ice Cream

Makes about 2 quarts

1¼ cups (250g) sugar

2 cups (472ml) heavy cream

1¼ cups (295ml) whole milk

4 large egg yolks

½ teaspoon kosher salt

1 cup (250g) peeled and smashed green-tipped bananas

I love the way the slight bitterness from the caramel balances the banana in this variation on a classic caramel ice cream. Bananas also aid in creating a smooth texture in the finished, frozen ice cream. Be careful. Once you start eating this, you may quickly end up with an empty container!

1. Fill a large bowl with ice cubes and cold water. Place a clean bowl inside it. Have a fine-mesh strainer handy.

2. Place a large light-colored saucepan over medium heat. When the pan has heated up a bit, add 1 cup of the sugar and 1 teaspoon of water. Cook over medium heat, stirring occasionally until the sugar has melted, about 3 minutes. Begin to swirl the pan gently as the sugar starts to caramelize. It will begin to brown in a few spots; when you see a few darker patches form, give the pan a swirl to spread the color out. Continue cooking until a dark amber caramel has formed, about 4 minutes more.

3. Turn the heat off and slowly add the heavy cream at arm's length, as it will bubble and spurt up the sides of the pan in steamy eruptions. Whisk the cream and caramel together. Return the mixture to medium heat until it boils vigorously and all the cream has been incorporated into the caramel, about 2 minutes. Add the milk and stir to combine.

4. Whisk together the egg yolks, remaining ¼ cup of sugar, and salt in a large heatproof bowl. Add a scant ¼ cup of the caramel cream to the yolks and whisk it in. Add the rest of the caramel mixture to the bowl and whisk to combine. Incorporating the hot liquid a little bit at a time tempers the eggs and helps prevent premature cooking or curdling. Pour the egg mixture into the saucepan and stir with a heatproof spatula. Cook over medium heat, stirring and scraping the bottom of the pan frequently, until it thickens to a custard and can coat the back of the spatula, about 5 minutes.

5. Strain the custard into the bowl set inside the ice bath. Add the bananas and whisk to combine. Chill the custard in the ice bath until it is very cold, about 40°F on an instant-read thermometer. Pour into the bowl of a 2-quart-capacity ice cream maker, and freeze according to the manufacturer's instructions.

6. Transfer the ice cream to an airtight container and chill it in the freezer for at least 4 to 5 hours before serving.

Green Melon and Tomato Granita

I first combined these two disparate characters in a gazpacho for a friend's late-summer wedding. Afterward the recipe was requested three times by various guests. A few years later I decided to turn the combination into a dessert-ish granita that could serve as both an after-dinner treat and a fancy cocktail-hour amuse-bouche. You can serve this with a shot of herbaceous gin and a splash of soda, which turns this green-on-green granita into an adult slushy. Just sayin'.

Makes about 2 quarts

1 pound (453g) ripe honeydew melon, seeded, peeled, and cut into 1-inch pieces

½ pound (227g) green zebra tomatoes, cored and coarsely chopped

⅓ cup (67g) sugar

1 handful fresh mint leaves

1 tablespoon fresh lemon juice

Place the honeydew, tomatoes, sugar, mint, and lemon juice in the carafe of a blender and puree on medium speed until the sugar has completely dissolved. Pour the mixture into a 13 x 9-inch dish. After 1 hour, check the granita to see if it has frozen. If it's not frozen enough to make shaved ice–like scrapes, return it to the freezer for another 30 minutes, or until it is solid. When you are ready to serve, use a large fork to scrape fluffy portions of granita, returning the granita to the freezer if it begins to melt. You can pre-scrape the granita 2 hours in advance, keeping it in an airtight container. It should retain its shaved fluffiness for that time, though it may be slightly crunchier in texture than fresh.

Peach Melba Sundaes

Makes 6 sundaes

2½ cups (500g) sugar

1 teaspoon vanilla bean paste or extract

3 medium ripe-but-firm peaches

2 cups (250g) fresh raspberries

2 tablespoons fresh lemon juice

1 recipe Brown Sugar Apricot Kernel Ice Cream (page 189)

Peach Melba—traditionally, poached peaches, raspberry sauce, and vanilla ice cream—is an old-timey classic that is deserving of a comeback. I have updated it with Brown Sugar Apricot Kernel Ice Cream. Prepare the various components in advance, then assemble after dinner and surprise your guests with a really elegant sundae. Break out the fancy crystal ice cream dishes for this one. It's worth it!

. . . .

1. Combine 2 cups of the sugar, the vanilla, and 2 cups (472ml) water in a medium saucepan over medium-low heat. Cook, stirring frequently, until the sugar dissolves. Wash the peaches and remove their skins using a vegetable peeler or paring knife. Cut the peaches in half, remove the pits, and add the peaches to the hot sugar syrup. Place the saucepan back on the heat and bring the peaches to a simmer over medium heat. Allow the mixture to simmer for 1 minute, then remove from the heat. Cool the peaches in the syrup. Store in an airtight container in the fridge until ready to serve.

2. Place the raspberries with the remaining ½ cup of sugar and the lemon juice in a blender and puree until smooth. Strain the puree through a fine-mesh strainer into a bowl; discard the seeds. Store the sauce in an airtight container in the fridge until ready to serve.

3. To assemble the sundaes, place half a peach in an ice cream dish and top with a generous scoop of ice cream. Drizzle the raspberry sauce over the ice cream. Enjoy immediately.

note: The Brown Sugar Apricot Kernel Ice Cream needs to be made 24 to 36 hours in advance.

Raspberry Campari Sorbet

Makes about 2 quarts

1½ cups (300g) sugar

2 pounds (906g) fresh ripe raspberries

3 tablespoons fresh lemon juice

¼ cup (59ml) Campari liqueur or Gran Classico Bitter

Pinch kosher salt

I am a sucker for bitter paired with sweet, and I choose my cocktails with that in mind. I had a wonderful Campari, gin, soda, and raspberry smash at a friend's house that inspired me to add a little Campari to my raspberry sorbet. A little alcohol makes for a smoother texture in frozen desserts. You could use neutral-flavored vodka instead, but the bitter note of Campari makes the raspberries in this frozen treat bounce with flavor.

1. Fill a large bowl with ice cubes and cold water and set a clean medium-size bowl inside it. In a small saucepan over medium heat, bring 2 cups (472ml) water to a boil, add the sugar, and stir. Continue cooking until the mixture is completely clear and all the sugar has dissolved, about 3 minutes. Remove the syrup from the heat and pour it into a heatproof bowl. Cool the syrup to room temperature.

2. In a blender, puree the raspberries with the syrup until smooth. Scrape the puree through a fine-mesh strainer into a bowl; discard the seeds. Stir the lemon juice, Campari, and salt into the raspberry puree and cool the fruit mixture in the ice bath until the mixture registers 40°F on an instant-read thermometer. Alternately you can cool the mixture to room temperature and refrigerate it overnight or for at least 6 hours.

3. Transfer the mixture into the bowl of a 2-quart ice cream maker. Freeze according to the manufacturer's instructions until almost set but still a little slushy, about 25 minutes.

4. Transfer the sorbet to an airtight container and chill it in the freezer until completely set, about 1 hour, before serving.

Sugared, Salted, and Preserved

Slow-Cooked Sour Apples

Slow-Cooked Rhubarb

Candied Citrus Zest

Olive Oil Lemon Curd

Preserved Meyer Lemons

Pear Shrub

Fruit Scrap Vinegar

Raspberry Cordial

Quinces Poached in Gin

Fermented Bananas

Strawberry Red Wine Jam

Sweet 100 Tomato Jam

Flavored Sugars

Slow-Cooked Sour Apples

Makes 3 cups

½ cup (100g) sugar

4 pounds (1812g) Pink Lady or Granny Smith apples, cored and cut into ⅛-inch slices

Slowly cooking the apples removes the liquid and concentrates the flavor. These are perfect in a pie, mixed 50/50 with fresh apples for texture.

Combine the sugar and ¼ cup (59ml) water in a large saucepan over medium heat. Cook until the sugar has melted, about 2 minutes. Add the apples and stir to coat in the sugar syrup. Cook, stirring often, until the apples are softened and translucent, about 25 minutes. Let cool completely before using. Store in an airtight container in the fridge for up to 2 weeks.

Slow-Cooked Rhubarb

·········

Makes 3 cups

·········

1 cup (200g) sugar

1 teaspoon vanilla bean paste or extract

2 pounds (906g) rhubarb, cut into
1-inch chunks

Cooking the rhubarb down over a low flame reduces the juices and fruit to a quick compote without the added sugar to make it a jam. It's a perfect compote to swirl into a tea cake batter and makes a zingy filling for a sponge cake.

···

1. Combine the sugar and vanilla in a large saucepan. You want the rhubarb to have plenty of space to cook gently. Add ½ cup (118ml) water and cook over medium heat, stirring occasionally, until the sugar melts, about 2 minutes. Add the rhubarb and stir to coat in the sugar syrup. Reduce the heat to low and cook, stirring occasionally but gently, until the rhubarb is softened and sticky, about 15 minutes. Let cool completely before using.

2. Store in an airtight container in the fridge for up to 2 weeks.

Candied Citrus Zest

3 oranges or lemons

1½ cups (300g) sugar, plus more for dredging (optional)

3 tablespoons honey

The aroma therapy you get from candying citrus is just one of the perks of making use of the whole fruit. Once you understand the basics of candying citrus, you can apply them to any citrus fruit. The method is simple enough: Slowly poach citrus peels in sugar syrup until they are cooked through and translucent.

1. Cut the citrus into wedges and remove the flesh. Use a sharp paring knife to remove as much white pith as possible from the peels. Reserve and use the insides of the fruits for juice or another use.

2. Place all the peels in a 2-quart saucepan. Cover the peels with water and bring them to a boil. Boil for 1 minute, then remove from the heat and drain. Set the peels aside.

3. Add the sugar, honey, and 1½ cups (354ml) water to the empty pan and bring to a simmer over medium heat. Cook to dissolve all the sugar, stirring frequently, about 7 minutes. Add the reserved peels to the sugar syrup and reduce the heat to low; gently simmer until the syrup registers 220°F on a candy thermometer or until the peels are bright and translucent looking. Stir the peels frequently. This should take about 1 hour. You do not want to caramelize the sugar at all, so keep the flame low and cook slowly. If the syrup begins to thicken before the peels have cooked through, you may need to add a touch more water to the pan during the cook time to slow down the candying process a bit.

4. Cool the peels in the syrup until they reach room temperature. From here you can go in two different directions: you can store the candied peels in an airtight container in the syrup to keep it soft and hydrated. Alternately, you can dredge the peels in granulated sugar and set them on a wire rack overnight to create a dried candied zest confection. The sugared zest can then be stored at room temperature for months and months.

note: Make sure to use unwaxed fresh fruit ONLY.

Olive Oil Lemon Curd

Makes 2 cups

¾ cup (150g) sugar

2 large whole eggs plus 3 large
  egg yolks

1 tablespoon freshly grated lemon zest

1 cup (236ml) fresh lemon juice
  (about 4 to 6 medium-size lemons)

2 teaspoons cornstarch

½ cup (118ml) extra-virgin olive oil

3 tablespoons unsalted butter, at room
  temperature

Use the best-quality peppery olive oil you can find for this curd. Because it has less butter, the finished product is slightly softer at room temperature than versions made with all butter, and the lemon flavor punches harder without the extra dairy. The cornstarch adds an extra measure of stiffness, so that the curd oozes a little bit less when it sits between cakes, and holds a perkier bead.

1. Fill a large bowl with ice cubes and cold water. Place a clean heatproof bowl inside it.

2. Combine the sugar, eggs and yolks, lemon zest, lemon juice, and cornstarch in a 2-quart heavy-bottomed saucepan and whisk them together. Cook over medium heat, stirring frequently with a wooden spoon or heatproof silicone spatula, until warm. Add the olive oil and butter and cook, stirring frequently, until the curd is thick enough to coat the back of the spoon, about 8 minutes.

3. Transfer the lemon curd to the bowl set inside the ice bath and cover with plastic wrap touching its surface. Chill until cold, at least 1 hour. Store in a sealed container in the fridge for up to 1 week.

Preserved Meyer Lemons

Makes 1 quart

6 to 8 Meyer lemons

1 cup (250g) fine sea salt

3 tablespoons raw turbinado sugar

2 cinnamon sticks

2 whole fresh or dried bay leaves

2 dried chiles de árbol

1 teaspoon whole black peppercorns

½ teaspoon coriander seeds

½ teaspoon fennel seeds

note: You can preserve lemons in just the salt and sugar. The spices are not required, but I highly recommended them. You can substitute Eureka or other lemon varieties for Meyer in equal measure.

The preserving process takes at least 1 month.

Every time I preserve citrus in salt and spices, I inhale very deeply and dream that one day a perfumer will bottle the scent of the fresh salt mix. The aroma is intoxicating and exotic and it smells like winter and summer at the same time. Its unstoppable brightness conjures the vision of lemonade stands in August and tangerines in Christmas stockings.

If you have friends with a lemon tree, or one of your very own, preserving lemons in salt will make great use of all that fruit. The recipe below is a guide, which can be expanded from a quart jar to as many jars as you need. You can try this recipe with limes, as my good friend Scarlett Lindeman does at her café Cicatriz in Mexico City. Scarlett preserves her limes with a similar spice blend but also adds fresh ginger. She uses the salty preserved limes in a broccoli dish.

My favorite use of preserved lemons is to drop half a rinsed, salty lemon into a pot of beans with a ton of olive oil. When the beans are fully cooked, the lemon has been simmered into a delicious softened treat that adds a bright note to the plate.

1. Wash a 1-quart jar with very hot water and allow it to air dry. Wash the lemons and trim the ends off each one. Cut a cross shape into the top of the lemon, slicing down three-quarters of the length of the fruit and creating quarters. Keep the bottom of the lemon intact.

2. In a large bowl, combine the salt, sugar, cinnamon, bay leaves, chiles, peppercorns, coriander, and fennel and toss with the lemons. Push the seasoned salt into the lemon segments and pack the lemons as tightly as possible into the prepared jar. Use a cocktail muddler or a wooden spoon to compact the lemons as much as possible.

3. Store the jar at room temperature with a loosely tightened lid. You can weigh the lemons down with a fermentation weight or a cup, but there isn't much need for that after the first week. They will release juices and the salt will begin to melt over time. The lemons will be ready after about 1 month of preserving, and will keep, stored in the refrigerator, for about 2 years. Always rinse off the lemons before using them, as they will be very salty. Both the flesh and the rind are edible.

Pear Shrub

Makes about 1 quart
undiluted shrub

1 pound (453g) ripe pears or fruit of
  your choice, cored and cut into
  1-inch chunks

2 cups (500g) raw turbinado sugar

2 cinnamon sticks

2 cardamom pods, cracked

1 teaspoon whole black peppercorns

2 cups (472ml) unfiltered apple cider
  vinegar

Sparkling water, for serving

Shrubs are simply a sweetened drinking vinegar that has been flavored with fruit and sometimes spices. They can be made with
any kind of ripe fruit, and served either on the rocks as a shot or
with sparkling water for a tart fruit soda. This recipe uses unfiltered raw vinegar that still contains the "mother" and has been
rumored to aid digestion thanks to the live probiotic of a vinegar
culture.

1. Combine the pears and sugar in a 2-quart saucepan over medium
heat. Add the cinnamon, cardamom, and peppercorns along with 1 cup
(236ml) water and bring the mixture to a simmer. Cook until all the sugar
has dissolved, stirring frequently, about 10 minutes. Remove the pan
from the heat and allow it to cool for 15 minutes. Add the vinegar. Let the
mixture steep at room temperature until the liquid is cool, then strain
out the pears and spices.

2. Serve ½ cup (118ml) of shrub syrup over ice, topped with 4 ounces of
sparkling water. Store the shrub in the fridge for up to 1 month.

Fruit Scrap Vinegar

Makes about 2 quarts

1 quart (944ml) distilled water

¼ cup (63g) raw turbinado sugar

1 pound (453g) fresh ripe fruit or scraps (apple and pear peels and cores, overripe soft fruits like peaches and nectarines), cut into 1-inch pieces (bruised is okay, but moldy is not)

I learned about the short path from juice to vinegar when I was just a kid. I opened a jug of fresh apple cider and heard an excited fizzy noise escape. I drank a gulp and was shocked at the boozy flavor. I brought the cider to my dad, and he explained that the cider had turned from juice to alcohol. Next stop would be vinegar.

This discovery fascinated me, and I began to notice this transformation more and more. During the late summer, birds and beetles would partake in fallen fruit and fly drunken paths across the yard. The fallen fruit turned to soured rot on the ground and resulted in a vinegary smell under the trees. I think this was the first "recipe" I knew by heart. When I started cooking for myself in college, I connected the dots and fell in love with vinegar.

Fruit scrap vinegar is a beautiful thing. It's easy to make, as long as you are curious, adventurous, and willing to wait. Brewing a batch of vinegar requires tasting and monitoring for the signs of fermentation. Once the sugars have turned to alcohol, the transition to vinegar can take weeks, and during those weeks you may become suspicious of the process. I question myself every time I start a new batch, until I taste the vinegar. For beginners I suggest fermenting the vinegar in a glass jar so you can monitor all the stages in the process. Once you're more comfortable with the process, and you have decided to devote some space in your life to brewing vinegar as well as cooking with it, invest in a beautiful ceramic vinegar crock.

If you have nurtured your fruity slop well, a healthy "mother" will form on the surface. In my experience, sometimes she's at the top of the container, but occasionally she will sink to the bottom as a milky-looking sediment. If it smells acidic, then you're on the right path. The mother is a good sign. It means you have created a mass of vinegar-making organisms.

1. Combine the water and sugar in a medium saucepan and bring to a simmer over medium heat. Stir frequently until the sugar has dissolved, about 3 minutes. Remove the pan from the heat and let the sugar syrup cool to room temperature.

recipe continues

note: It's best to make vinegars in cooler times of the year, as extreme heat speeds up the process and can make it difficult to control the fermentation.

The vinegar-making process takes at least 1 month and can take longer.

2. While the sugar syrup cools, place the fruit in a 3-quart glass or ceramic crock. An apple core or a few greens from berries can go into the jar, too, as long as they have not been sprayed with pesticides. I like to include a leaf from whatever fruit variety I'm working with; I believe that the naturally occurring yeast from the outdoors helps start my vinegar off on the right foot.

3. Pour the cooled syrup over the fruit. Cover the top of the jar with cheesecloth or a clean towel (to allow for air to come in) and secure it with a rubber band. Air is a sort of ingredient in vinegar making, and the mixture needs air to be able to ferment. Place the jar out of direct sunlight in a temperate part of the kitchen (you want someplace not too cold but no hotter than 75°F).

4. Stir the fruit once daily for 1 week. You may see bubbles or hear fizzing when you stir the fruit. If so, taste the liquid to confirm the presence of alcohol. (You may also be able to smell it and detect the booziness—if it smells boozy, it has turned to alcohol.) Strain the fruit out and discard it. Replace the cheesecloth and band and leave the jar undisturbed for another week.

5. From here it's a wait-and-see game. Check the jar, but do not stir it. Look for a glob of whitish jelly floating—that's the mother. If she's arrived, you're really doing this vinegar thing right! Some fruit produces a thicker floating mother (peaches and nectarines), while others (apples, cherries, blackberries) produce a finely textured sediment or a thin film of culture on the surface of the liquid. So much depends on the environment, and there is no one right look. It's all about reading the signs.

6. Smell and taste the vinegar again and again over the next few weeks. Stop when you think it tastes great, depending on how strong you want the vinegar to be. If it tastes like vinegar, and has no booziness at all, then it is indeed vinegar.

7. When the vinegar is ready, remove the solid mother from it to use for a new batch. The mother will mature with age, getting stronger from batch to batch and increasing the complexity of the vinegar each time. Cover the fruit vinegar with a solid lid and refrigerate indefinitely. Left unshaken, it will separate over time, but just shake it up before you use it and you're good to go. Held at room temperature, it may grow another mother, and over time it might become less potent. Storing it in the fridge extends this time.

8. How should you use it? Make a salad! Add some honey and soda water and make a shrub! Take a shot of it in the morning to jump-start your gut. Save fruit scraps in the freezer in between batches and make use of all the stuff that would normally end up in the compost.

Raspberry Cordial

....

Makes about 2½ cups

....

2 cups (250g) fresh raspberries

2 cups (472ml) applejack brandy
 (I like Laird's Jersey Lightning)

Wide 1-inch strip lemon peel

Simple syrup, for serving

Sparkling wine or club soda, for serving
 (optional)

The cordial can be used in a variety of ways and makes a wonderful gift for those who imbibe. If you keep it in the freezer, it pours like a light syrup from the jar and makes a nice boozy drizzle for vanilla ice cream.

. . . .

1. Combine the raspberries, brandy, and lemon peel in a 1-pint mason jar and seal tightly. Let sit in a cool, dark place, shaking the jar every few days until the mixture is a deep red color, about 1 month.

2. Strain the mixture through cheesecloth and into a pitcher or large bowl. Do not press on the solids, or the mixture will become cloudy. Add simple syrup to taste.

3. Serve the cordial in small glasses. To make a spritzer, place 2 tablespoons of the cordial in a flute and top it off with sparkling wine. You can store the cordial in the refrigerator for up to 6 months, as long as the lid remains tightly closed. With time the flavor will continue to round out and become smoother, though it is ready to use after the initial month's time.

note: It is important to keep air out of the jar. As I discussed in the fruit vinegar recipe (page 217), air allows for the fermentation process to continue and you will begin to make vinegar.
 The cordial-making process takes at least 1 month and can take longer.

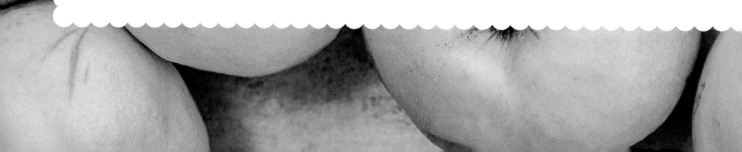

Gin and Quinces

One fall season a friend left a box of apples and quinces for me at another friend's cheese shop. This is the kind of wonderful life I live. People leave gifts of fruit in places they know I will stop by, boxes with my name written in black marker "FOR RUCKER" containing interesting things they grew at home and want to share. They know I will get them, and use them. I brought the box of fruit home, made apple butter with rose petals, and left the quinces on the kitchen counter in an emerald-green glass dish, hoping to experience firsthand the ancient aroma of ripening quinces.

Over the next week, a smell began to waft from that corner of the kitchen. The quinces seemed to be glowing in the green glass bowl—almost like a living still-life painting. I had never left quinces out to ripen at home, but historically a bowl of quinces left at room temperature was a form of aroma therapy in many old-world houses. It's hard enough to get quinces at all in Los Angeles. The trees don't seem suited to our climate, and quinces aren't edible right off the tree—they need

to go through an additional ripening (or bletting, more accurately; see page 13 for more about the ripening process). And quinces need to be cooked for a very long time before they resemble anything edible. This has made them inconvenient and, in modern times, an unattractive garden addition.

Many quince lovers and writers refer to an Andalusian-Arabic poem by Shafer ben Utman al-Mushafi about quince that describes the aroma seductively:

It has the perfume of a loved woman and the same hardness of heart, but it has the colour of the impassioned and scrawny lover.
Its pallor is borrowed from my pallor; its smell is my sweetheart's breath.

It's as indescribable as that. The aroma is so distinct but also so hard to put your finger on an accurate likeness. It's sweet, honey-like, and musky. It smells like apples and pears comingling with a pineapple. Some days, the quinces reminded me of a certain bottle of gin I had hiding in my collection, a gin that I found to be too sweet for a martini and had mostly forgotten about until the quinces brought it back to mind.

I have a respectable gin collection, more than I should own, being that I am not really a drinker. I love a good martini, especially a briney one, but I don't often mix a cocktail for myself at home. I think I started collecting gin because of the botanical aromas each different bottle contains. One bottle has rose and juniper, another bottle smells like pine needles and apple peels—they're all so different.

So, on the day I was supposed to turn in a finished manuscript of recipes and stories about fruit, I decided to write one more recipe. I peeled the quinces and drowned them in aromatic gin and raw sugar, and added a vanilla bean. (Another gift, from a friend of a friend in Mexico City—I have great friends!) I topped the pot off with water and sat down to go over my manuscript, checking commas and making last-minute adjustments. Soon I was surrounded by the warm perfume of poaching quinces, and an hour later I treated myself to a slice of soft, pink fruit still steaming from the gin bath.

The alcohol had completely cooked away, and what was left was a warm, old-fashioned, complex flavor bomb. The syrup from the pot was pure ambrosia, and the quinces had been poached to a richly textured, reddish-pink jewel. I stashed them away in a jar, and used a few slices here and there throughout the winter until I had half the jar left. I decided to use them all in one last blast: an epic quince dessert for a potluck. I tucked them in between slices of apples inside flaky pie dough to create one of the best galettes I've ever made; the smell of the galette was so powerful as it cooled, it was everything I could do to not cut right into it while it was still hot.

After dinner I watched as several guests enjoyed it for dessert. There was a lot of competition on the potluck table, and at the end of the party there were several slices left on the plate. The polite guests passed it by in favor of some chocolate bliss balls or something else more on trend. When it came time to leave, I quietly collected my plate and the remaining slices with it. I wasn't planning on leaving my precious quince dessert on the pile of potluck leftovers!

Buy five or six large yellow quinces, preferably leaves attached. Arrange them in your nicest fruit bowl or on a lovely platter, and place them in a well-ventilated part of your kitchen or dining room. Wait for the ancient romantic aromas to fill the room. Boil them in some sweet syrup and stash them away for a rainy day.

Quinces Poached in Gin

Makes 2 quarts

1 vanilla bean, split in half lengthwise

6 ripe quinces (906g), peeled, quartered, and cored

2 cups (500g) raw turbinado sugar

1 cup (236ml) delicious, aromatic gin

Poached fruit is wonderful served for breakfast alongside granola and yogurt. The gin-poached quinces keep for a long time in the fridge and make a great last-minute dessert served with ice cream and a little drizzle of the poaching syrup.

1. Scrape the seeds from the vanilla bean and combine the seeds and the pod with the quinces, sugar, and gin in a large heavy-bottomed saucepan. Add 4 cups (944ml) water to the pan and bring the mixture to a rolling boil over medium heat. Reduce the heat to a simmer. Cut a piece of parchment paper to cover the surface and poke one hole in the center of the paper. Place the parchment on the surface of the fruit and cook until the quinces are fork tender and the liquid and flesh of the fruit has turned a tawny rose color, about 2 hours. Add more water if necessary to keep the quinces floating freely.

2. Using a slotted spoon, remove the quinces from the liquid and place in a bowl. Continue to simmer the liquid over medium heat until it's reduced to a light syrup, about 15 minutes. Pour the reduced syrup and the vanilla bean over the quinces and let cool to room temperature. Refrigerate the quinces in the syrup, leaving the vanilla bean in the mixture. They will keep this way in a sealed container for up to 4 months.

Fermented Bananas

Makes about 3 cups

8 medium (453g) very ripe bananas, peeled

2 tablespoons raw turbinado sugar

If you love bananas, like I do, this is a fun project to push the boundaries of what the flavor of a banana is. Bananas are often pegged as sweet and one-dimensional—filler for smoothies or a soft food for toothless babies to snack on—but I think bananas get a bad rap. Fermenting the banana takes the flavor and aroma to a complex and tropical place. Once the alcohol has dissipated a little bit, the aroma is very similar to a wheaty beer.

1. Fermenting bananas can take between 3 and 7 days, so it's best to start this project about 1 week before you want to use fermented bananas in any recipe.

2. Mash the bananas with the sugar in a glass or ceramic bowl. Cover the bowl with a clean kitchen towel held in place with a rubber band or a piece of string tied around the bowl, and keep in a dark part of the kitchen at warm room temperature (75°F).

3. Check the bananas after 24 hours. The surface of the mash should have darkened a little bit; this is not the same as mold; it is simply oxidization. If mold is present, the fermentation has gone too far and the mixture needs to be discarded. I have never had the process get to that point. Continue to stir the banana mash twice daily, looking for signs of fermentation—bubbling or fizzing when the mash is agitated. The bananas are ready once they're bubbly and give off a beer-like aroma. Stir the banana mash well, as it will have separated during the fermentation. Use right away or store in the freezer until needed, making sure to thaw the bananas in the fridge overnight before you use them.

note: This recipe calls for very ripe bananas, so make sure they're just that— browning with black, speckled peels.

Strawberry Red Wine Jam

....

Makes eight ½-pint jars

....

3 pounds (1359g) fresh strawberries, cleaned, hulled, and quartered

3 cups (600g) sugar

1 cup (236ml) fruity red wine, such as Merlot, Beaujolais, or Zinfandel

½ cup (118ml) fresh lemon juice (about 2 to 3 medium-size lemons)

Adding a cup of fruity red wine elevates the comforting flavor of strawberry jam to a complex, grown-up preserve. It makes the perfect filling for a classic sponge cake, and because the alcohol is cooked out completely, it also makes a very sophisticated toast at breakfast.

....

1. Combine the berries and sugar in a large nonreactive pot and mash them together with a potato masher or fork. Add the red wine and bring the mixture to a simmer over medium heat. Transfer the mixture to a heatproof bowl, cover tightly with plastic, and rest at room temperature overnight.

2. The next day, preheat your oven to 225°F. Place a clean plate and four metal spoons in the freezer. Wash eight ½-pint jars and lids, place them open side up on a baking sheet, and keep them warm in the oven while you cook the jam.

3. Bring the strawberry mixture to a boil over medium-high heat in a large nonreactive pot, such as a copper jam pan. Add ¼ cup of the lemon juice to the jam. Continue to boil the jam, scraping and stirring often, until the foam from the jam subsides, about 15 minutes. Add the remaining ¼ cup of lemon juice and continue to boil for another 10 minutes. Remove the jam from the heat, and let the bubbling subside.

4. Test the jam's doneness by scooping a small spoonful of jam onto a cold spoon from the freezer. Place the cold spoon on the cold plate and return them to the freezer for 1 minute. After 1 minute, the jam should be thickened and leave a trail when you drag a finger through it. If the jam has not thickened enough, return the pot to the heat and continue to boil for another 2 minutes. Remove the jam from the heat and test it again; look for jam that is hesitant to drip on the spoon.

5. If you plan to can the jam, proceed immediately. Remove the jars and lids from the oven (leave the oven on) and divide the jam among the jars. Secure the lids. Place the full jars upright on the baking sheet and bake for 15 minutes. Remove the jars from the oven and cool them on a wire rack, leaving at least 1 inch between them. As the jars come to room temperature, the button in the canning lid will suction inward, making a popping sound. This is the sign of a properly sealed jar of jam. Any jars of jam that do not pop have not been sealed and should be kept in the fridge, where they keep well for 3 months. The sealed strawberry jam keeps well for 1 year at room temperature.

note: Make the base for the jam 1 day in advance to allow it to rest overnight.

Sweet 100 Tomato Jam

....

Makes about 4 cups

·········

2 pounds (906g) ripe cherry tomatoes,
cleaned and stemmed

½ cup (100g) sugar

1 tablespoon sherry vinegar

1 teaspoon sea salt

Sweet 100 tomatoes are the jewels of the summer tomato glut. We grow them every year, and when they begin to ripen in long cascades of color, the game is on to use every single one of them before the birds get them. I spend several hours a week slowly cooking them in olive oil with garlic, herbs, and spices. The sweetest and juiciest of the crop always get made into this unusual oven jam. Spiked with sherry vinegar to nudge the jam toward a savory note, this is fantastic with aged cheddar and good bread.

. . . .

1. Position a rack in the center of your oven and preheat the oven to 350°F.

2. Cut one-third of the tomatoes in half. Then combine all the tomatoes, sugar, vinegar, and salt in a 13 x 9-inch ovenproof dish. Place the tomatoes in the oven and cook, stirring every 20 minutes, until the juices thicken and the tomatoes begin to caramelize, about 1 hour. Remove the dish from the oven and let the sticky tomato jam cool to room temperature. Store in a sealed container in the fridge for up to 1 month. This jam is not safe for canning.

note: Instead of firing up a traditional oven, I often use a toaster oven that has a roast setting for stress-free cooking that won't turn the summer kitchen into a hot hell.

Flavored Sugars

When I think of making flavored sugars and storing them for future baking projects, I imagine myself as a sort of potion maker. Mixing a little of this and a little of that, storing it, and pulling it out later to match with a fruit or a custard base.

Vanilla Bean

2 vanilla bean pods,
(you can use pods that
have been previously
scraped of their seeds)
2 cups (400g) sugar

When you use the seeds from a vanilla bean pod for cookies or custard, you are left with an empty seed pod. Keep this "discarded" pod in the freezer. It should never, ever be thrown in the trash! The price of vanilla beans and the length of time required to get from flower to extract makes them one of the most valuable edible commodities on the planet, and we must use every inch of the pod to honor its journey.

Lay the pods on a baking sheet and dry them slowly in a 200°F oven or a dehydrator for about 1 hour. Once they are brittle and dried, combine them in a food processor with 1 cup of sugar per bean pod. Pulse the machine until you have a well-speckled sugar. Sift out any larger, unprocessed pieces if you like a more uniform sugar. I prefer to leave them all in and pick them out if I'm making a cookie or cake with the sugar.

You can use this flavored sugar for anything you would use vanilla and sugar in. Substitute it cup for cup in your recipe but omit the vanilla paste or extract in the recipe, as the sugar will be potently perfumed. Keeps indefinitely.

Citrus

1½ cups (300g) sugar
1 tablespoon freshly grated
citrus zest

In the bowl of a food processor, combine the sugar and zest and pulse the machine until you have a well-speckled sugar. Substitute this flavored sugar cup for cup in citrus curds or cake recipes, or use it to roll sugar cookies in. If you are using the citrus sugar in a recipe that also calls for zest, omit the zest in the recipe. Store at room temperature for up to 1 week, or keep the sugar in the freezer indefinitely.

Lavender, Rose, or Fennel

1½ cups (300g) sugar

1 tablespoon dried culinary lavender flowers, rose petals, or fennel seeds or pollen

In the bowl of a food processor, combine the sugar and the lavender flowers, rose petals, or fennel seeds or pollen. Pulse the machine until you have a speckled sugar. Sift out any larger, unprocessed pieces if you'd like a more uniform sugar. I prefer to leave them all in and pick them out if I am making a cookie or cake with the sugar.

Use this flavored sugar to season fruit tarts or pie fillings, or to roll sugar cookies in. I would suggest substituting this sugar for only one-fourth of the total sugar in your recipe, as it will be strongly perfumed and could overpower the recipe. Keeps indefinitely.

Herbal Sugar

1½ cups (375g) raw turbinado sugar

½ cup dried rose geranium leaves/flowers (leaves washed and dried well), lemon verbena, basil, rosemary, or thyme

In the bowl of a food processor, combine the sugar and herb and pulse the machine until you have a well-speckled sugar. Sift out any larger, unprocessed pieces if you desire a more uniform texture. You can substitute this flavored sugar cup for cup in ice cream bases, cake batters, and fruit pie fillings, or for rolling sugar cookies in. Keeps indefinitely.

Pantry Recipes

Granola

Flaky Butter Crust

Flaky Whole-Wheat Crust

Pasta Frolla

Pistachio Pasta Frolla

Brioche Dough

Ricotta Biscuits

Crème Anglaise

Pastry Cream

Simple Sugar Glaze

Almond Cream

Pistachio Cream

Granola

....

Makes about 6 cups

....

1¼ cups (295ml) grade A dark
  maple syrup

¾ cup (177ml) grapeseed oil

½ cup (100g) packed dark brown sugar

1 tablespoon vanilla bean paste
  or extract

½ teaspoon ground cinnamon

½ teaspoon kosher salt

2 cups (180g) old-fashioned rolled oats

2 cups (180g) rye flakes

1 cup (150g) raw almonds

½ cup (100g) raw sunflower seeds

½ cup (100g) raw pepitas

3 tablespoons black sesame seeds

1. Position two racks in the center zone of your oven and preheat the oven to 325°F. Line two large baking sheets with parchment paper.

2. Combine the maple syrup, grapeseed oil, brown sugar, vanilla, cinnamon, and salt in a heavy-bottomed saucepan. Bring the mixture to a simmer over medium heat, simmer for 2 minutes, then remove the mixture from the heat.

3. In a large heatproof bowl, toss together the remaining ingredients. Add the hot maple syrup mixture. Stir with a heatproof spatula or wooden spoon until every piece of seed and grain has been coated with the syrup.

4. Divide the granola and spread over the two prepared baking sheets. Bake for 15 minutes undisturbed, then carefully stir once every 15 minutes for 1 hour. Rotate the pans top to bottom and front to back at the 45-minute mark. Bake until the grains are toasted and the granola has a golden-brown color and dry texture. Cool the granola completely before storing in a sealed container at room temperature for up to 1 month.

Flaky Butter Crust

....

*Makes two 9½-inch single crusts
or 1 double crust with some dough
left over for lattice work
or other decoration*

....

¼ cup (50g) packed dark brown sugar

1 tablespoon unfiltered apple cider
   vinegar

1½ teaspoons fine sea salt

4 cups (500g) all-purpose flour,
   plus more for the surface

3 sticks (339g) unsalted butter,
   cold and cut into ½-inch cubes

When I set out to develop my own pie dough recipe, I scoured my cookbook collection for unique recipes from which to find inspiration. There were so many recipes, all claiming to be the "flakiest," "butteriest," "best ever," but most of them followed a traditional formula of cold fat, cold flour, and cold water. Some recipes called for vinegar, others swore by vodka. The vinegar intrigued me, mainly because I love vinegars and have quite a collection of them—a vinegar for every kind of recipe calling for acid.

When I dug further into the vinegar lead, I found that two recipes containing vinegar came out with excellent results. Though both needed tweaks to make them my own and adjust them to my taste, they each resulted in shattering flakes with great butter flavor and uniform color. One of the recipes was from Bourke Street Bakery in Sydney, Australia—and in that recipe, the authors actually dissolve the sugar in the water with the vinegar.

This was a lightbulb moment—dissolving the sugar in the liquid with vinegar creates a syrup that permeates the dough thoroughly. The color after baking is intense and the flavor and aroma of the cooked crust is a dish all its own.

Making pie goes back hundreds of years. The basic ratio of fat to flour wavers very little from recipe to recipe and the technique remains mostly the same, but the addition of vinegar adds a layer of tenderizing magic that shortens the production of gluten strands. Gluten is a friend in pie dough, but too much gluten makes for an inedible brick.

I prefer to use a vinegar with flavor, like unfiltered apple cider vinegar, as well as dark brown sugar for even more flavor and caramelization. Brown sugar is also considered to be an acid, and so it has similar tenderizing abilities as the vinegar, which means that this pie dough recipe is incredibly forgiving and has become one of my most consistent recipes. The raw pie dough tastes seasoned, as it should in my opinion.

You can make pie dough with your hands, you can cut the fat into the flour with a pastry cutter, you can squish the butter chunks into the flour with a rolling pin—there are as many methods for incorporating fat into flour as there are bad pie

recipe continues

dough recipes. I stand by my simple pinch and smear method, and though there are plenty of ways to shortcut things, the hand-made method works the best for me and for the team of bakers that make perfect pies at my bakery. I think that you can tell the difference between a hand-processed crust and a machine-processed crust. A crust made by hand will have a texture that is tender, and the outer edge will have visible layers and flakes when you cut into the slice.There will be less uniformity, but that's the charm of a pie.

. . . .

1. In a measuring cup, combine the brown sugar, vinegar, and salt with ¾ cup (107ml) of hot water. Stir until the sugar has dissolved. Chill the liquid in the freezer until it is very cold (this should take about 20 minutes) and leave it in the fridge until you are ready to start the rest of the dough.

2. Combine the flour and half of the butter in a large mixing bowl. Pinch and smear the butter between your fingers. Processing the butter like this creates small leaves of butter that layer in the dough, resulting in flakes later. Once all the butter chunks have been pinched, grab small handfuls of flour and butter and rub the two together between the palms of your hands until the mixture resembles uneven pebbles on a sandy beach.

3. Dump the crumbly mixture out onto a lightly floured work surface. Scatter the remaining half of the cold butter over the dough. Use the palm of your hand to smear the butter as if you were sliding a secret message across a table. Use a bench scraper to gather the shaggy dough and repeat the smearing process until you have a pile of striated rubble. The larger pieces of butter will create a marbled dough and will melt during baking, causing the water in the butter to evaporate (this will result in flaky pastry pockets).

4. Gather the buttery mixture up in a mound and form a well in the center. Remove the cold liquid from the fridge and pour half of it into the well. Using your fingertips, slowly bring the flour and butter into the center and combine it with the liquid until the liquid has been incorporated. Gather the moistened dough into a pile.

5. Slowly pour the remaining liquid onto the shaggy mess. Lift the dough from the bottom and squeeze just until it comes together into one mass. Divide the ball in half and shape each half into a disc. Wrap each in plastic and chill for 2 hours before using.

Flaky Whole-Wheat Crust

Makes two 9½-inch single crusts or 1 double crust with some dough left over for lattice work or other decoration

....

5 tablespoons (63g) packed dark brown sugar

1 tablespoon unfiltered apple cider vinegar

1½ teaspoons fine sea salt

4 cups (480g) whole-wheat pastry flour

3 tablespoons all-purpose flour, plus more for the surface

3 sticks (339g) unsalted butter, cold and cut into ½-inch cubes

I offer this whole-wheat pie dough variation with the confidence that if you use freshly milled whole-wheat flour, the results will be fantastic and complex in flavor. I have used whole-grain spelt, wheat, and einkorn flours with great results.

1. In a measuring cup, combine the brown sugar, vinegar, and salt with ¾ cup (107ml) of hot water. Stir until the sugar has dissolved. Chill the liquid in the freezer until it is very cold (this should take about 20 minutes) and leave it in the fridge until you are ready to start the rest of the dough.

2. Combine the whole-wheat flour, all-purpose flour, and half of the butter in a large mixing bowl. Pinch and smear the butter between your fingers. Processing the butter like this creates small leaves of butter that layer in the dough, resulting in flakes later. Once all the butter chunks have been pinched, grab small handfuls of flour and butter and rub the two together between the palms of your hands until the mixture resembles uneven pebbles on a sandy beach.

3. Dump the crumbly mixture out onto a lightly floured work surface. Scatter the remaining half of the cold butter over the dough. Use the palm of your hand to smear the butter as if you were sliding a secret message across a table. Use a bench scraper to gather the shaggy dough and repeat the smearing process until you have a pile of striated rubble. The larger pieces of butter will create a marbled dough and will melt during baking, causing the water in the butter to evaporate (this will result in flaky pastry pockets).

4. Gather the buttery mixture up in a mound and form a well in the center. Remove the cold liquid from the fridge and pour half of it into the well. Using your fingertips, slowly bring the flour and butter into the center and combine with the liquid until the liquid has been incorporated. Gather the moistened dough into a pile.

5. Slowly pour the remaining liquid onto the shaggy mess. Lift the dough from the bottom and squeeze just until it comes together into one mass. Divide the ball in half and shape each half into a disc. Wrap each in plastic and chill for 2 hours before using.

Pasta Frolla

*Makes two 9-inch single tart crusts,
with extra dough for
trimming and repairs*

3¼ cups (406g) all-purpose flour,
plus more for the surface

¾ cup (150g) sugar

¼ teaspoon kosher salt

1 stick (113g) unsalted butter, cold and
cut into ½-inch cubes

2 large eggs

1½ teaspoons freshly grated lemon zest

¼ teaspoon vanilla bean paste
or extract

Pasta frolla is an Italian shortcrust pastry dough. Unlike American pie dough, it is meant to be tender and consistent in texture. It uses the strength and richness of eggs to achieve its signature golden color and prevent the dough from shrinking during baking. Often the dough is flavored with lemon and/or vanilla, as it is in my recipe. The result is a buttery cookie-like tart dough that is incredibly forgiving, especially during rolling.

1. In the bowl of a food processor fitted with the blade attachment, combine the flour, sugar, and salt and pulse the machine three times to combine. Add the butter and pulse five times in 1-second bursts. Then, while running the motor of the machine, add the eggs, lemon zest, and vanilla and continue mixing until a smooth dough forms.

2. Transfer the dough to a lightly floured work surface. Break off a golf ball–size piece of dough, put it under the heel of your hand, and slide and smear the ball of dough forward on the work surface a couple of inches. Scrape up the dough, set it aside, and repeat with the remaining dough, 1 portion at a time. This technique is called *fraisage* and is a traditional method used to incorporate butter into shortcrust pastry by smearing the dough after you've mixed it. You elongate the pieces of butter. Instead of butter chunks, you end up with butter that's streaked throughout the structure of the dough.

3. Scrape the dough up into a mound and divide it into 2 discs. Wrap each disc in plastic and chill for 30 minutes before using.

note: Pasta frolla is often rolled out between two sheets of parchment paper and then transferred to the baking dish. This makes the soft dough easier to handle, but does not guarantee that the dough will transfer in one piece. It may break or crack in places, but the dough is designed to be pressed back together or even patched up without any loss of structure. You can essentially treat this dough as you would a crumb crust if you wish, pressing and smoothing it into your tart pan.

Pistachio Pasta Frolla

....

Makes two 9-inch single tart crusts,
with extra dough for
trimming and repairs

....

2¾ cups (344g) all-purpose flour,
    plus more for the surface

¾ cup (150g) sugar

1 cup (95g) fine-ground pistachios

¼ teaspoon kosher salt

1 stick (113g) unsalted butter, cold and
    cut into ½-inch cubes

2 large eggs

1½ teaspoons freshly grated lemon zest

¼ teaspoon vanilla bean paste
    or extract

This variation on the traditional pasta frolla uses ground pistachios for a speckled and delicious effect. I like to use this nut-enriched dough for stone-fruit tarts, as I love the flavors of pistachios and butter with bright acidic apricots, plums, or cherries. Alternately, this dough makes a wonderful shortbread cookie that is sturdy enough to sandwich with jam.

. . . .

1. In the bowl of a food processor fitted with the blade attachment, combine the flour, sugar, pistachios, and salt. Pulse the machine three times to combine. Add the butter and pulse the machine five times in 1-second bursts to incorporate. Then, while running the motor of the machine, add the eggs, lemon zest, and vanilla and continue mixing until a smooth dough forms.

2. Transfer the dough to a lightly floured work surface. Break off a golf ball–size piece of dough, put it under the heel of your hand, and slide and smear the ball of dough forward on the work surface a couple of inches. This technique is called fraisage and is a traditional method used to incorporate butter into shortcrust pastry by smearing the dough after you've mixed it. You elongate the pieces of butter. Instead of butter chunks, you end up with butter that's streaked throughout the structure of the dough.

3. Scrape up the dough, set it aside, and repeat with the remaining dough, one portion at a time. Gather the dough up into a mound and divide it into 2 discs. Wrap each disc in plastic and chill for at least 30 minutes before using.

note: Pasta frolla is often rolled out between two sheets of parchment paper and then transferred to the baking dish. This makes the soft dough easier to handle, but does not guarantee that the dough will transfer in one piece. It may break or crack in places, but the dough is designed to be pressed back together or even patched up without any loss of structure. You can essentially treat this dough as you would a crumb crust if you wish, pressing and smoothing it into your tart pan.

Brioche Dough

Makes 12 doughnuts or buns

⅓ cup (79ml) warm whole milk

1¾ teaspoons active dry yeast

2¾ cups (349g) bread flour

3 tablespoons sugar

1 large whole egg plus 3 large egg yolks

¾ teaspoon kosher salt

½ teaspoon vanilla bean paste or extract

2 tablespoons unsalted butter, at room temperature, plus more for greasing the bowl

This is my all-purpose brioche dough, used for making doughnuts and sweet buns. If you'd like to use it for a savory application, omit the vanilla.

1. In a small bowl, combine the milk and yeast with ⅓ cup (79ml) warm water, stirring until the yeast dissolves. Let the mixture sit in a warm place until it begins to foam, about 5 minutes.

2. In the bowl of an electric mixer fitted with the dough hook attachment, combine the flour, sugar, and the foamy yeast mixture. Start the motor on low speed and add the egg, egg yolks, salt, and vanilla.

3. Continue mixing on low speed just until the dough starts to come together. Turn the motor off and allow the dough to sit inside the mixer for 15 minutes. Return the mixer to low speed and slowly add the butter 1 tablespoon at a time. After both additions of butter, mix until the butter has been totally incorporated into the dough, about 5 minutes. This slow-mixing technique is how you get the silky, strong brioche dough structure. Increase the speed to medium and mix until the dough is smooth and elastic, 15 to 20 minutes. It will be slightly sticky but shouldn't tear easily.

4. Lightly grease a large bowl. Put the dough inside and cover with plastic wrap. Let the dough rise in the fridge overnight, or up to 24 hours, before proceeding with the desired recipe.

5. You can also make the dough up to 2 weeks in advance and freeze it. Then, before you would like to use it in a recipe, thaw the dough in the fridge overnight.

note: This recipe really requires the use of an electric stand mixer. You should not attempt to make this by hand.

Ricotta Biscuits

Makes 16 biscuits

5 cups (500g) cake flour, plus more
   for rolling

3 tablespoons sugar

1 tablespoon baking powder

2 teaspoons baking soda

2 teaspoons kosher salt

2 sticks (226g) unsalted butter, cold
   and cut into ½-inch cubes

2 cups (472ml) cold buttermilk, plus
   more for brushing

1½ cups (372g) cold whole-milk ricotta
   cheese, drained for at least 1 hour in
   a fine-mesh strainer lined with two
   layers of cheesecloth

Something magical happened the day I decided to dump a container of fresh ricotta into my standard biscuit recipe. I thought I would get lumps and layers of cheese in the biscuits, but I got something better than that. The ricotta melts into the biscuit in most places and creates a fluffy crumb that I had been trying to achieve for years but never knew the secret to. These are dangerously addictive. Proceed with caution.

1. Sift the flour, sugar, baking powder, baking soda, and salt into a large mixing bowl. Place the bowl in the freezer to chill for 20 minutes.

2. Add the butter to the dry ingredients and toss to combine. Pinch and smear the pieces of butter between your fingers. Processing the butter like this creates small leaves of butter that layer in the dough, resulting in flakes later. Once all the butter chunks have been pinched, grab small handfuls of flour and butter and rub the two together between the palms of your hands until the mixture resembles uneven pebbles on a sandy beach.

3. Create a well in the center of the mixture and add 1 cup of the buttermilk. Using a fork, toss the flour and butter from around the edge of the well into the center. Fluff the buttermilk and flour mixture with the fork five or six times, until shaggy looking.

4. Crumble the ricotta cheese into tablespoon-size chunks over the dough, making sure not to break up the cheese too much. Using your hands with your fingers spread wide open, loosely incorporate the cheese into the dough with a lift-and-gently-squeeze motion. Drizzle the remaining 1 cup of buttermilk over the dough while using the fork to bring the mixture together into a loose and shaggy mass.

5. Scrape the dough onto a lightly floured work surface and use your hands to shape the dough into a 10 x 7-inch rectangle. Fold the rectangle in thirds like a letter and then rotate 90 degrees. Using a rolling pin, flatten the dough back into a 10 x 7-inch rectangle. Repeat the folding, rotating, and rolling process two more times, ending with the dough shaped into a 10 x 7-inch rectangle of about 1-inch thickness. Wrap the dough with plastic and refrigerate for 30 minutes.

recipe continues

6. Position two racks in the center zone of your oven and preheat the oven to 400°F. Line two baking sheets with parchment paper.

7. Return the dough to the work surface and roll it out into a 12 x 10-inch rectangle of about ¾-inch thickness. Using a sharp knife, trim and discard ¼ inch from all sides of the dough. Cut the rectangle into 4 evenly spaced vertical strips, and then into 4 horizontal strips to get 16 biscuits. Place 8 biscuits about 1½ inches apart on each prepared baking sheet. Generously brush the tops of the biscuits with buttermilk.

8. Bake until the biscuits are golden brown and have expanded upwards to reveal fluffy layers on the sides, 18 to 20 minutes. Cool for as long as you can stand it, or risk a burned mouth and go for it.

Crème Anglaise

....

Makes about 2 cups

....

4 large egg yolks

3 tablespoons sugar

1 cup (236ml) whole milk

½ cup (118ml) heavy cream

1 teaspoon vanilla bean paste or extract

1. Fill a large bowl with ice cubes and cold water. Place a clean heatproof bowl inside it. Set a fine-mesh strainer over the heatproof bowl.

2. In a separate heatproof bowl, combine the egg yolks and sugar and whisk until the mixture is pale yellow and creamy looking; you can use an electric mixer for this step if you want. Set aside.

3. Combine the milk, cream, and vanilla in a medium heavy-bottomed saucepan. Cook over medium heat until steam rises from the surface, about 5 minutes.

4. Pour a quarter of the hot milk into the egg mixture and whisk to incorporate. Add the remaining milk mixture and whisk it in. Transfer the mixture back to the pan and cook over medium heat, whisking constantly, until the custard coats the back of a spoon, 4 to 6 minutes.

5. Quickly pass the custard through the strainer into the heatproof bowl. Cover the crème anglaise with plastic wrap, pressing the plastic directly onto the surface to prevent a skin from forming, and cool it completely in the ice bath. The sauce can be made ahead and kept in the refrigerator, covered with plastic wrap, for up to 3 days.

Pastry Cream

......

Makes about 4 cups

......

1 large whole egg plus 4 large egg yolks

½ cup (100g) sugar

3 tablespoons cornstarch

¼ teaspoon salt

3 cups (708ml) whole milk

1 teaspoon vanilla bean paste or extract

1 stick (113g) unsalted butter,
  cut into 8 pieces, cold

1. Fill a large bowl with ice cubes and cold water. Place a clean heatproof bowl inside it. Set a fine-mesh strainer over the heatproof bowl.

2. In a separate heatproof bowl, whisk together the whole egg, egg yolks, sugar, cornstarch, and salt until just incorporated. Set aside.

3. Combine the milk and the vanilla in a medium heavy-bottomed saucepan. Cook over medium heat until the milk simmers. Remove the pan from the heat.

4. While whisking, pour one-quarter of the hot milk into the egg mixture and whisk to incorporate. Add the remaining milk mixture slowly, whisking to combine. Transfer the mixture back to the pan and cook over medium heat, stirring and scraping the bottom of the pan with a heatproof spatula, until the custard is thick and bubbles appear in the center, 4 to 6 minutes.

5. Using the spatula, quickly pass the custard through the strainer into the heatproof bowl. Add the butter 1 tablespoon at a time, whisking until the butter has been totally incorporated.

6. Cover the pastry cream with plastic wrap, pressing the plastic directly onto the surface to prevent a skin from forming, and cool it completely in the ice bath. The pastry cream can be made ahead and kept in the refrigerator, covered with plastic wrap, for up to 3 days.

Simple Sugar Glaze

......

Makes about 1 cup

......

1½ cups (188g) confectioners' sugar

1 teaspoon vanilla bean paste or extract

¼ teaspoon kosher salt

Whisk the confectioners' sugar, vanilla, salt, and 2 tablespoons of hot water until very smooth. Add small splashes of water, as needed, to reach a thick, honey-like consistency.

Almond Cream

Makes about 1½ cups

1 stick (113g) unsalted butter,
  at room temperature

½ cup (100g) sugar

1 large egg

¼ teaspoon almond extract

Pinch kosher salt

1 cup (96g) almond flour

In the bowl of an electric mixer, beat together the butter and sugar on medium speed until very light and fluffy, about 3 minutes. Add the egg, almond extract, and salt and beat until incorporated. With the machine off, add the almond flour, then mix at medium speed until no dry bits of almond flour remain. If you're not going to use the almond cream immediately, transfer the cream to an airtight container and keep it in the fridge for up to 1 week.

Pistachio Cream

Makes about 1½ cups

1 stick (113g) unsalted butter,
  at room temperature

½ cup (100g) sugar

1 large egg

¼ teaspoon almond extract

Pinch salt

1 cup (100g) fine-ground pistachios

In the bowl of an electric mixer, beat together the butter and sugar on medium speed for about 3 minutes, until very light and fluffy. Add the egg, almond extract, and salt and beat until incorporated. Turn the machine off and add the pistachios. Mix at medium speed until no dry bits of pistachios remain. If you're not going to use the almond cream immediately, transfer the cream to an airtight container and keep it in the fridge for up to 1 week.

Acknowledgments

I cry easily, especially when counting my blessings, so by the end of this I will be a mess. There are so many people who have helped make this book come to life! My husband, Blaine Rucker, for choosing to put up with my requests for more fruit trees and plants and doing all the hard manual labor, and in general being the best partner. My family, especially my parents, for always encouraging my obsessions. My team (my work family, listed alphabetically, not by favorites; you are all my favorites): Ian Amparo, Erik Black, Sergio Espana, Arik Nagel, Alex Rose, Krystle Shelton, and Tamara Vasquez. My friend Shawn Pham, a talented chef who tested many of the recipes and left me excruciatingly detailed notes. My trusted advisers and friends who also happen to be talented writers—Gillian Ferguson and Scarlett Lindeman. The farmers! The farmer's market produce master Karen Beverlin, who will text with me for hours discussing apples. This book would not exist without Nicole Tourtelot, Pam Krauss, and the guidance and care of everyone at Avery—Lucia Watson and her team, thank you. Extra-special thanks for Lydia Clarke and Alan Gastelum, who spent far too many hours with me fussing over plates and light and made the most beautiful book.

Index

Page numbers in *italics* refer to photos.

A

almonds, almond flour, almond cream
  Almond and Berry Cobbler, *120*, 121
  Almond Cream, 247
  Apricot Almond Polenta Cake, *46*, 47
  Apricot Bostock, 20, *21*
  Banana Cream Pie, *144*, 145–46
  Cherry Almond Meringue Clouds, 73
  Chewy, Nutty, Fruity Granola Bars, 74
  Granola, *232*, 233
  Pear Financiers, 69
  Spiced Tangerine Semolina Cake, *78*, 79–80, *81*
  Sweet Wine and Fruit Cake, *82*, 83
apples
  Apple Brown Betty, 118, *119*
  Apple Crumb Slab Pie, 142, *143*
  Dutch Baby with Sautéed Apple Compote, *26*, 27
  Fruit Soup, 28
  Slow-Cooked Sour Apples, 207
  Sour Apple Pie, 138–41, *139*
  Spiced Apple Wedding Cake, *90*, 91–92
  Apricot Kernel Brown Sugar Ice Cream, *188*, 189
apricots
  Apricot Almond Polenta Cake, *46*, 47
  Apricot Bostock, 20, *21*
  Apricot Galette, *180*, 181–82
  Fruit Soup (dried apricots), 28
Avocado Pistachio Pound Cake with Lemon Glaze, *50*, 51

B

Backyard Citrus Upside-Down Cake, 84, *85*
bananas
  Banana Buckwheat Cake, *42*, 43
  Banana Cream Pie, *144*, 145–46
  Caramel Banana Ice Cream, 197
  Fermented Banana Cake, 52, *53*
  Fermented Bananas, 223
  Magic Banana Pudding Cake, 93
bars. See cookies and bars
basic recipes. See also pantry recipes
  Candied Citrus Zest, *210*, 211
  Citrus Sugar, 228
  Fermented Bananas, 223
  Flavored Sugars, 228–29
  Fruit Scrap Vinegar, *216*, 217–18
  Herbal Sugar, 229
  Lavender, Rose, or Fennel Sugar, 229
  Olive Oil Lemon Curd, 212, *213*
  Pear Shrub, 215
  Preserved Meyer Lemons, 214
  Quinces Poached in Gin, 222
  Raspberry Cordial, 219
  Slow-Cooked Rhubarb, 208, *209*
  Slow-Cooked Sour Apples, 207
  Strawberry Red Wine Jam, 224, *225*
  Sweet 100 Tomato Jam, 227
  Vanilla Bean Sugar, 228
berries. See also raspberries; strawberries
  Almond and Berry Cobbler, *120*, 121
  Berry and Bran Muffins, *22*, 23
  Berry Buttermilk Pie, 147–48, *149*
  Black and Blue Pie with Brown Sugar Crumb, *150*, 151
  Blackberry Frozen Yogurt, 194
  Boysenberry Hand Pies, 154
  Coffee and Croissant Bread Pudding, 99
  Huckleberry Blondies, 63
  Pear and Cranberry Pie, 164, *165*
  Summer Pudding, 110, *111*
  Sweet Corn Pudding with Blackberries, *108*, 109
Betty, Apple Brown, 118, *119*
Biscuits, Ricotta, 242–44, *243*
Black and Blue Pie with Brown Sugar Crumb, *150*, 151
blackberries. See berries
Black Raspberry Ice Cream, 190, *191*
Blondies, Huckleberry, 63
blueberries. See berries
Boiled Maple "Pumpkin" Pie, *170*, 171–72
Bostock, Apricot, 20, *21*
Boysenberry Hand Pies, 154
Bran and Berry Muffins, *22*, 23
Bread Pudding, Coffee and Croissant, 99
breakfast and brunch recipes
  Apricot Almond Polenta Cake, *46*, 47
  Apricot Bostock, 20, *21*
  Avocado Pistachio Pound Cake with Lemon Glaze, *50*, 51
  Banana Buckwheat Cake, *42*, 43
  Berry and Bran Muffins, *22*, 23
  Carrot and Pineapple Cake with Coconut Glaze, 48, *49*
  Dutch Baby with Sautéed Apple Compote, *26*, 27
  Fermented Banana Cake, 52, *53*
  Fruit Soup, 28
  Jam-Filled Doughnuts, 33–34, *35*
  Mango Coconut Bundt Cake, *54*, 55
  Multi-Grain Porridge and Pear Pancakes, 24, *25*
  Plum and Yogurt Soufflé Cake, 44, *45*
  Raspberry Scones, *18*, 19

breakfast and brunch recipes *(cont.)*
  Rhubarb Coffee Cake with
    Browned Butter Streusel, *38,*
    39–40, *41*
  Sour Lemon Cakes, 56, *57*
  Strawberry Brioche Danishes with
    Fromage Blanc, *30,* 31–32
  Strawberry Rye Buckle with Rose
    Hazelnut Crumb, 36–37
  Sweet Corn and Raspberry
    Muffins, *58,* 59
Brioche Danishes with Fromage
  Blanc, Strawberry, *30,* 31–32
Brioche Dough, *240,* 241
Brownies, Raspberry Halva, *60,* 62
Buckle, Strawberry Rye, with Rose
  Hazelnut Crumb, 36–37
Buckwheat Cake, Banana, *42, 43*
Bundt Cake, Mango Coconut, *54,* 55
Buttermilk Berry Pie, 147–48, *149*

C

cakes
  Apricot Almond Polenta Cake, *46,*
    47
  Avocado Pistachio Pound Cake
    with Lemon Glaze, *50,* 51
  Backyard Citrus Upside-Down
    Cake, 84, *85*
  Banana Buckwheat Cake, *42, 43*
  Carrot and Pineapple Cake with
    Coconut Glaze, 48, *49*
  Fermented Banana Cake, 52, *53*
  Flourless Chocolate and Pear
    Spoon Cake, 100, *101*
  Isabel's Lemon Birthday Cake, *86,*
    87–88, *89*
  Magic Banana Pudding Cake, 93
  Mango Coconut Bundt Cake, *54,* 55
  Plum and Yogurt Soufflé Cake,
    44, *45*
  Spiced Apple Wedding Cake, *90,*
    91–92
  Spiced Tangerine Semolina Cake,
    78, 79–80, *81*
  Strawberry Cornmeal Shortcake,
    94, *95*
  Strawberry Rye Buckle with Rose
    Hazelnut Crumb, 36–37
  Swedish Cream Buns with
    Strawberries, *96,* 97–98

Sweet Wine and Fruit Cake, *82,* 83
Candied Citrus Coconut Macaroons,
  64, *65*
Candied Citrus Zest, *210,* 211
Caramel Banana Ice Cream, 197
Caramelized Pineapple Tarts, 173
Carrot and Pineapple Cake with
  Coconut Glaze, 48, *49*
Cheesecake, Provençal-Style, 183–84,
  185
Cherimoya and Green Tea Ice Cream,
  196
cherries
  Baked Vanilla Custard with
    Berries, *102,* 103
  Cherry Almond Meringue Clouds
    (dried cherries), 73
  Chewy, Nutty, Fruity Granola Bars,
    74
chocolate
  Cherry Almond Meringue Clouds,
    73
  Flourless Chocolate and Pear
    Spoon Cake, 100, *101*
  Raspberry Halva Brownies, *60,* 62
citrus fruit. *See also* lemons
  Candied Citrus Coconut
    Macaroons, 64, *65*
  Candied Citrus Zest, *210,* 211
  Citrus Flavored Sugar, 228
  Lime Pie That Saved Us, The, 168,
    169
  Rhubarb and Blood Orange
    Pavlova, *130,* 131–32
  Spiced Tangerine Semolina Cake,
    78, 79–80, *81*
  Whole Tangerine Sorbet, *192, 193*
Cobbler, Almond and Berry, *120, 121*
Cobbler, Peach and Ricotta Biscuit,
  122, *123*
Coconut Candied Citrus Macaroons,
  64, *65*
Coconut Glaze, Carrot and Pineapple
  Cake with, 48, *49*
Coconut Mango Bundt Cake, *54,* 55
Coffee and Croissant Bread Pudding,
  99
Coffee Cake, Rhubarb, with Browned
  Butter Streusel, *38,* 39–40, *41*
cookies and bars
  Candied Citrus Coconut
    Macaroons, 64, *65*

Cherry Almond Meringue Clouds,
  73
Chewy, Nutty, Fruity Granola Bars,
  74
Huckleberry Blondies, 63
Krystle's Lemon Ginger Cookies,
  65, 66–67
Orange-Anise Cookies (variation),
  67
PB&J Thumbprint Cookies, *65,* 68
Pear Financiers, 69
Pistachio Ginger Linzer Cookies,
  70, 71–72
Raspberry Halva Brownies, *60,* 62
Sour Cream Fig Bars, 75
Strawberry-Coconut Cookies
  (variation), 67
Cordial, Raspberry, 219
Corn and Raspberry Muffins, *58,*
  59
Cornmeal Strawberry Shortcake,
  94, *95*
Corn Pudding with Blackberries,
  108, 109
Cranberry and Pear Pie, 164, *165*
Cream Buns with Strawberries,
  Swedish, *96,* 97–98
Crème Anglaise, 245
Crisp *or* Crumble *but Not* Cobbler,
  126, *127*–28
Curd, Olive Oil Lemon, 212, *213*
Custard with Berries, Baked
  Vanilla, *102,* 103

D

Danishes, Strawberry Brioche, with
  Fromage Blanc, *30,* 31–32
Doughnuts, Jam-Filled, 33–34, *35*
Dutch Baby with Sautéed Apple
  Compote, *26,* 27

F

Fermented Banana Cake, 52, *53*
Fermented Bananas, 223
figs, dried
  Fruit Soup, 28
  Sour Cream Fig Bars, 75
  Sweet Wine and Fruit Cake, *82, 83*
figs, fresh, *in* Roasted Fig Frozen
  Yogurt, 195

Financiers, Pear, 69
Flavored Sugars, 228–29
Flourless Chocolate and Pear Spoon
    Cake, 100, *101*
Fromage Blanc, Strawberry Brioche
    Danishes with, *30*, 31–32
frozen desserts. *See also* ice cream
    Blackberry Frozen Yogurt, 194
    Green Melon and Tomato Granita,
        198, *199*
    Raspberry Campari Sorbet, 202,
        203
    Roasted Fig Frozen Yogurt, 195
    Whole Tangerine Sorbet, *192*, 193
fruit, to choose, 13–15
Fruit Crisp *or* Crumble *but Not*
    Cobbler, *126*, 127–28
Fruit Scrap Vinegar, *216*, 217–18
Fruit Soup, 28

G

Galettes, Apricot, *180*, 181–82
Galettes, Strawberry, 178, *179*
Ginger and Pear Strudel, 114–17, *115–16*
Ginger Cookies, Krystle's Lemon, *65*,
    66–67
Ginger Linzer Cookies, Pistachio, *70*,
    71–72
Glaze, Simple Sugar, 246
Granita, Green Melon and Tomato,
    198, *199*
Granola, *232*, 233
Granola Bars, Chewy, Nutty, Fruity, 74
Green Melon and Tomato Granita,
    198, *199*
Green Tea and Cherimoya Ice Cream,
    196

H

Halva Raspberry Brownies, *60*, 62
Hand Pies, Boysenberry, 154
Hazelnut Rose Crumb, Strawberry
    Rye Buckle with, 36–37
Herbal Sugar, 229
Honey-Glazed Strawberry Pie, *166*,
    167–68
Huckleberry Blondies, 63

I

ice cream
    Black Raspberry Ice Cream, 190,
        191
    Brown Sugar Apricot Kernel Ice
        Cream, *188*, 189
    Caramel Banana Ice Cream, 197
    Cherimoya and Green Tea Ice
        Cream, 196
    in Peach Melba Sundaes, *200*, 201

J

Jam, Strawberry Red Wine, 224, *225*
Jam, Sweet 100 Tomato, 227
Jam-Filled Doughnuts, 33–34, *35*
July Flame Peach Pie, 152, *153*

L

Lavender, Rose, or Fennel Sugar, 229
lemons
    Backyard Citrus Upside-Down
        Cake, 84, *85*
    Frankie's Lemon Pie, *160*, 161
    Isabel's Lemon Birthday Cake, *86*,
        87–88, *89*
    Krystle's Lemon Ginger Cookies,
        65, 66–67
    Olive Oil Lemon Curd, 212, *213*
    Preserved Meyer Lemons, 214
    Sour Lemon Cakes, 56, *57*
Lime Pie That Saved Us, The, 168, *169*
Linzer Cookies, Pistachio Ginger, *70*,
    71–72

M

Macaroons, Candied Citrus Coconut,
    64, *65*
Magic Banana Pudding Cake, 93
Mango Coconut Bundt Cake, *54*, 55
Melon and Tomato Granita, Green,
    198, *199*
Meringue Clouds, Cherry Almond, 73
Meyer Lemons, Preserved, 214
Muffins, Berry and Bran, *22*, 23
Muffins, Sweet Corn and Raspberry,
    58, 59
Multi-Grain Porridge and Pear
    Pancakes, 24, *25*

O

Olive Oil Lemon Curd, 212, *213*
oranges. *See* citrus fruit

P

Pancakes, Multi-Grain Porridge and
    Pear, 24, *25*
pantry recipes. *See also* basic recipes
    Almond Cream, 247
    Brioche Dough, *240*, 241
    Crème Anglaise, 245
    Flaky Butter Crust, 234–36, *235*
    Flaky Whole-Wheat Crust, 237
    Granola, *232*, 233
    Pasta Frolla, 238
    Pastry Cream, 246
    Pistachio Cream, 247
    Pistachio Pasta Frolla, 239
    Ricotta Biscuits, 242–44, *243*
    Simple Sugar Glaze, 246
Passion Fruit Posset, 107
Pasta Frolla, 238
Pasta Frolla, Pistachio, 239
Pastry Cream, 246
Pavlova, Rhubarb and Blood Orange,
    130, 131–32
PB&J Thumbprint Cookies, *65*, 68
peaches
    July Flame Peach Pie, 152, *153*
    Peach and Ricotta Biscuit Cobbler,
        122, *123*
    Peach Melba Sundaes, *200*, 201
pears
    Flourless Chocolate and Pear
        Spoon Cake, 100, *101*
    Multi-Grain Porridge and Pear
        Pancakes, 24, *25*
    Pear and Cranberry Pie, 164, *165*
    Pear and Ginger Strudel, 114–17,
        115–16
    Pear Financiers, 69
    Pear Shrub, 215
    Vanilla Rice Pudding with
        Marsala-Baked Pears, 104–6,
        105
pie crusts
    Flaky Butter Crust, 234–36, *235*
    Flaky Whole-Wheat Crust, 237
    Pasta Frolla, 238
    Pistachio Pasta Frolla, 239

pies and tarts
    Apple Crumb Slab Pie, 142, *143*
    Apricot Galette, *180,* 181–82
    Banana Cream Pie, *144,* 145–46
    Berry Buttermilk Pie, 147–48, *149*
    Black and Blue Pie with Brown
        Sugar Crumb, *150,* 151
    Boysenberry Hand Pies, 154
    Caramelized Pineapple Tarts, 173
    Frankie's Lemon Pie, *160,* 161
    Honey-Glazed Strawberry Pie, *166,*
        167–68
    July Flame Peach Pie, 152, *153*
    Lime Pie That Saved Us, The, 168, *169*
    Pear and Cranberry Pie, 164, *165*
    Provençal-Style Cheesecake,
        183–84, *185*
    Prune and Pistachio Cream Tart,
        176, 177
    Rhubarb Pie, *156,* 157–58, *159*
    Rhubarb Tarte Tatin, 174, *175*
    Sour Apple Pie, 138–41, *139*
    Strawberry Galettes, 178, *179*
    Sweet 100 Turnovers, 155
Pineapple and Carrot Cake with
    Coconut Glaze, 48, *49*
Pineapple Tarts, Caramelized, 173
pistachios, pistachio flour, pistachio
    cream
    Avocado Pistachio Pound Cake
        with Lemon Glaze, *50,* 51
    Pear Financiers, 69
    Pistachio Cream, 247
    Pistachio Ginger Linzer Cookies,
        70, 71–72
    Pistachio Pasta Frolla, 239
    Prune and Pistachio Cream Tart,
        176, 177
Plum and Yogurt Soufflé Cake, 44, *45*
Polenta Cake, Apricot Almond, *46,* 47
Porridge and Pear Pancakes, Multi-
    Grain, 24, *25*
Posset, Passion Fruit, 107
Pound Cake, Avocado Pistachio, with
    Lemon Glaze, *50,* 51
Provençal-Style Cheesecake, 183–84,
    185
Prune and Pistachio Cream Tart, *176,*
    177
Pudding Cake, Magic Banana, 93
puddings
    Apple Brown Betty, 118, *119*
    Baked Vanilla Custard with
        Berries, *102,* 103
    Coffee and Croissant Bread
        Pudding, 99
    Passion Fruit Posset, 107
    Summer Pudding, 110, *111*
    Sweet Corn Pudding with
        Blackberries, *108,* 109
    Tomato Pudding, 112, 113
    Vanilla Rice Pudding with Marsala-
        Baked Pears, 104–6, *105*
"Pumpkin" Pie, Boiled Maple, *170,*
    171–72

Q

Quinces Poached in Gin, 222

R

raspberries
    Black Raspberry Ice Cream, 190, *191*
    Peach Melba Sundaes, *200,* 201
    Raspberry Campari Sorbet, 202,
        203
    Raspberry Cordial, 219
    Raspberry Halva Brownies, *60,* 62
    Raspberry Scones, *18,* 19
    Summer Pudding, 110, *111*
    Sweet Corn and Raspberry
        Muffins, *58,* 59
rhubarb
    Rhubarb and Blood Orange
        Pavlova, *130,* 131–32
    Rhubarb Coffee Cake with
        Browned Butter Streusel, *38,*
        39–40, *41*
    Rhubarb Pie, *156,* 157–58, *159*
    Rhubarb Tarte Tatin, 174, *175*
    Slow-Cooked Rhubarb, 208, *209*
Rice Pudding, Vanilla, with Marsala-
    Baked Pears, 104–6, *105*
Ricotta Biscuit and Peach Cobbler,
    122, *123*
Ricotta Biscuits, 242–44, *243*
Roasted Fig Frozen Yogurt, 195

S

Scones, Raspberry, *18,* 19
Semolina Cake, Spiced Tangerine, *78,*
    79–80, *81*

Shortcake, Strawberry Cornmeal,
    94, *95*
Shrub, Pear, 215
Slab Pie, Apple Crumb, 142, *143*
Slow-Cooked Rhubarb, 208, *209*
Slow-Cooked Sour Apples, 207
Sorbet, Raspberry Campari, 202, *203*
Sorbet, Whole Tangerine, *192,* 193
Soufflé Cake, Plum and Yogurt, 44, *45*
Soup, Fruit, 28
Sour Apple Pie, 138–41, *139*
Sour Cream Fig Bars, 75
Sour Lemon Cakes, 56, *57*
Spiced Apple Wedding Cake, 90, 91–92
Spiced Tangerine Semolina Cake, *78,*
    79–80, *81*
Spoon Cake, Flourless Chocolate and
    Pear, 100, *101*
strawberries
    Baked Vanilla Custard with
        Berries, *102,* 103
    Chewy, Nutty, Fruity Granola Bars
        (dried strawberries), 74
    Honey-Glazed Strawberry Pie, *166,*
        167–68
    Provençal-Style Cheesecake,
        183–84, *185*
    Strawberry Brioche Danishes with
        Fromage Blanc, *30,* 31–32
    Strawberry Cornmeal Shortcake,
        94, *95*
    Strawberry Galettes, 178, *179*
    Strawberry Red Wine Jam, 224, *225*
    Strawberry Rye Buckle with Rose
        Hazelnut Crumb, 36–37
    Summer Pudding, 110, *111*
    Swedish Cream Buns with
        Strawberries, *96,* 97–98
Strudel, Pear and Ginger, 114–17, *115–16*
Sugars, Flavored, 228–29
Summer Pudding, 110, *111*
Sundaes, Peach Melba, *200,* 201
Swedish Cream Buns with
    Strawberries, *96,* 97–98
Sweet Corn and Raspberry Muffins,
    58, 59
Sweet Corn Pudding with
    Blackberries, *108,* 109
Sweet 100 Tomato Jam, 227
Sweet 100 Turnovers, 155
Sweet Wine and Fruit Cake, *82,* 83

T

tangerines. *See* citrus fruit
Tarte Tatin, Rhubarb, 174, *175*
tarts. *See* pies and tarts
Thumbprint Cookies, PB&J, *65*, 68
tomatoes
    Green Melon and Tomato Granita,
      198, *199*
    Sweet 100 Tomato Jam, 227
    Sweet 100 Turnovers, 155
    Tomato Pudding, *112*, 113
Turnovers, Sweet 100, 155

U

Upside-Down Cake, Backyard Citrus,
   84, *85*

V

Vanilla Bean Sugar, 228
Vanilla Custard with Berries, Baked,
   102, 103
Vanilla Rice Pudding with Marsala-
   Baked Pears, 104–6, *105*
Vinegar, Fruit Scrap, *216*, 217–18

W

Whole Tangerine Sorbet, *192*, 193
Wine and Fruit Cake, *82*, 83
Wine Jam, Strawberry, 224, *225*

Y

Yogurt, Blackberry Frozen, 194
Yogurt, Roasted Fig Frozen, 195
Yogurt and Plum Soufflé Cake, 44, *45*